T0319209

Perspectives of Labour Migration from Mzimba District, Malawi, to South Africa

Harvey Chidoba Banda

Langaa Research & Publishing CIG
Mankon, Bamenda

Publisher
Langaa RPCIG
Langaa Research & Publishing Common Initiative Group
P.O. Box 902 Mankon
Bamenda
North West Region
Cameroon
Langaagrp@gmail.com
www.langaa-rpcig.net

Distributed in and outside N. America by African Books Collective
orders@africanbookscollective.com
www.africanbookscollective.com

ISBN-10: 9956-762-23-7

ISBN-13: 978-9956-762-23-1

Dedication

For
Harry Chidoba Banda (Father),
Edith Njikho (Mother)
and
Gladwell Nthara (Former Migrant)!

Table of Contents

Acknowledgements

This book has taken an inordinately long time to produce. This is largely a result of pressure of work at Mzuzu University, where there is hardly time, throughout the year, during which to embark on such an uphill task: the conventional academic programme is followed by the open and distance programme, which largely takes centre-stage during the semester breaks. For those academic members of staff, like myself, who take part in both programmes, the situation on the ground borders on what I might describe as 'academic torture' or 'imprisonment without knowing'. In spite of this cloud of uncertainty, I have to mention that in writing this book, I drew inspiration from a number of authors, one of whom being Dr Ignasio M. Jimu of the Geography Department at Mzuzu University, especially after the novel publication of his book *Urban Appropriation and Transformation: Bicycle Taxis and Handcart Operators in Mzuzu, Malawi* (2008).

It is common knowledge that writing a book is a herculean and pains-taking task and more so when one is combining it with the already-demanding academic work. Hence it is through zeal and determination that in 2016 I authored my first book *Vidokoni: Folktales from Mzimba, Malawi*. But still something kept on urging me to forge ahead and publish a book on the social history of labour migration from Malawi to South Africa. This book, 'a smokescreen', is a direct outcome of this internal urge.

If I am to borrow Belinda Bozzoli's formulation in her book *Women of Phokeng: Consciousness, Life Strategy, and Migrancy in South Africa, 1900-1983* (1991), this book, *Perspectives of Labour Migration from Mzimba District, Malawi, to South Africa*, was completed in the comparatively peaceful milieu of

Witwatersrand University, where the History Department provided a base which was quite convenient for the arduous and torturous task of writing. Although I had embarked on this book project while at Mzuzu University, before embarking on my doctoral studies, pressure of work forced me to shelve it 'indefinitely'. It was during my doctoral studies that I decided, out of whimsicality, to revive the project. This was strange, indeed, taking cognizance of the amount of academic work that was before me. Colleagues and friends in South Africa like Joshua Kumwenda, Lameck Khonje, Elijah Wanda (all from Mzuzu University, Malawi), and Vusumuzi "Vusi" Khumalo (South African) helped to create a tranquil environment: the hearty jokes during pass-times and the encouragement to embark on such academic pursuits as publishing despite our busy schedules 'turbo-charged' me with unparalleled determination.

A word of thanks should also go to the many interviewees who gave generously of their time for the research (oral interviews) on which the chapters in this book are based. It is sad that most of these interviewees will never see this book (the ultimate outcome of the oral interviews), but, it is my hope, some of them, or their descendants, will benefit from the development of inter-state and migration policies that may arise from it. I will be doing great injustice if I do not single out a few of these informants: Charles Makamo, a former migrant, who over the years played the role of a lead informant and guide during interviews in Zubayumo Makamo area, one of the major labour migration areas in Mzimba District; Wilson Banda (my brother), who doubled as my Research Assistant and informant. Through his interaction with his friends-cum-migrants, he provided useful insights on labour migration from the district. Last but not least, Gladwell Nthara stands out of them all in many respects. Gladwell, through his insistence, granted me an interview while he was sickly by forcing himself out of the bed! "You are doing a noble cause; our labour migration experiences in South Africa ought to be documented for the benefit of our children and those yet unborn and for posterity", Gladwell maintained. It is with sadness that I learnt of his passing a few years later. It is, therefore, with heartfelt sympathy that I partly dedicate this book to him. May the soul of Gladwell Nthara rest in peace!

I am profoundly grateful to my wife, Jennifer Luhanga, whose tolerance and forbearance during my frequent and extended absences from home are rare. As for my son, Owen, I hope this second book settles his humorous scepticism about my academic abilities regarding authorship. Above all, I owe a great debt of gratitude to my parents, Harry Chidoba Banda and Edith Njikho, for their inquisitive minds about my academic pursuits and their sole wish that I reach the highest echelons of the academic ladder was an 'incessant drive' in me to forge ahead. It is, therefore, in order that this book is dedicated to them.

Preface

Human history is the history of migration. People have been involved in moving from one area to another since time immemorial. These movements are orchestrated by different reasons. Broadly, migrations occur under two main strands: First, voluntary migrations where people move out of choice and for different reasons, for instance, looking for wage employment (labour migration) and also for trade purposes (commercial migration). Second, involuntary migrations or forced migrations where people are forced to move from their areas of habitual residence due to circumstances beyond their control, for example, due to wars, earthquakes and floods.

In the case of Malawi, migrants generally come under voluntary migration. Historically, Malawi has generally been peaceful, with people being compelled to emigrate to other countries and regions due to lack of income-earning opportunities. During the colonial period, that is, at the end of the 19th century and during the first half of the 20th century, the people in Malawi (then Nyasaland) relied heavily on subsistence farming for survival, with a cross-section securing wage employment on plantations and estates in the Shire Highlands region. With time, Malawians learnt about better wage employment opportunities obtaining in such countries as Zimbabwe (Southern Rhodesia), Zambia (Northern Rhodesia), and South Africa. In these countries, they were largely working in the mines.

This book is on the nature of labour migration from Malawi, broadly, and Mzimba District, specifically, since the late 19th century. It shows that between the 1880s and 1980s Malawians were emigrating either informally (*selufu*) or formally (under *Wenela* and later *Theba*). The book advances the argument that the decline in mine migrancy directly or indirectly led to the increase in informal labour migration (*selufu*). What is more, the book shows that during the post-1990 period, this labour migration became exclusively informal. It also shows that although labour migrants faced challenges during the pre-1990 period, they faced more and complicated challenges during the post-1990 period. However, using the human agency theory, the book fervently argues that Malawian labour migrants make rational and informed decisions whether to emigrate or not in the midst of these challenges.

Harvey C. Chidoba Banda
Witwatersrand University, 2017

Chapter 1

Introduction

1.   Landscape of Labour Migration History from Malawi

Malawians have been emigrating for wage employment not only to South Africa, but also to Zambia and Zimbabwe for more than one hundred years. However, of these countries, the majority of migrant workers were destined for South Africa. Labour migration to the latter country dates back to the discovery of diamond and gold between 1850 and 1900. Diamond was discovered in 1867 in Kimberley whereas gold was discovered in 1886 in the Witwatersrand (Yudelman 1984: 19; Jeeves et. al 1991: 2). This was followed by the establishment of diamond and gold mines, respectively. Since mining diamond and gold was labour intensive, the South African mines, henceforth, were in dire need of man power to exploit the precious minerals. This development led to the consequent influx of people looking for wage employment on these mines. Although initially it was local South Africans who provided the much-needed labour on these mines, within a short period of time word spread far and wide about the availability of better-paying jobs on the mines.

In Malawi (then Nyasaland) missionaries belonging to different groupings like the Dutch Reformed Church Mission, the Free Church of Scotland, the Established Church of Scotland, and the Catholic Missions established mission stations in different parts of the country between 1850 and 1900 (McCracken 2012). In addition to teaching the word of God, they also established schools where converts were taught basics in reading, writing and counting. All this was part of what they referred to as 'the civilizing mission'.[1] The Free Church of Scotland moved their mission station from Cape Maclear to Bandawe in Nkhata-Bay in 1881 and thereafter opened schools in the area (Pachai 1973: 17).

After successfully maintaining peace between the Ngoni of Mzimba and the Tonga of Nkhata-Bay, the Livingstonia Mission (of the Free Church of Scotland) concentrated on education and evangelization. A fair number of the earliest African Christian converts were the Tonga. By 1894 there were eighteen schools in Tongaland and over 1,000 pupils in regular attendance. In 1906 there were 107 schools with over 3,500 pupils (Pachai 1973: 21).

Consequently, some Tonga men attained basic education. Thereafter, they started looking for jobs in the Shire Highlands. It is these missionaries who alerted them about higher-paying jobs in the South African mines (Coleman 1972; Pachai 1973: 21). This marked the beginning of a long history of labour migration from Malawi from the 1890s onwards.

The labour migration history from Malawi to South Africa can be categorized into two clear-cut periods: the old labour migration period from the 1880s to the 1980s, and the new migration period or contemporary period, from the 1990s onwards (Banda 2008). During the old migration period, labour migration took two forms: official migration or contract migration and informal migration, popularly known as *selufu*[2] in Malawi. It is noteworthy that migrants started emigrating to South Africa under *selufu* since formal migration started a few years later after the formation of labour recruiting agencies. The Witwatersrand Native Labour Association (WNLA), popularly known as *Wenela* was formed in 1897 with the aim of recruiting labour from outside South Africa, while the Native Recruiting Corporation (NRC) was formed in 1912 to mastermind the recruitment of domestic labour (James 1992: 1).

Under the South African labour historiography, the old labour migration period (1880s-1980s) may be further subdivided into three clear-cut and smaller phases based on the nature of labour migration, the numbers of labour migrants involved and the role of the state in controlling labour migration. The first phase starts from the 1880s to the 1920s. This is regarded as the formative stage. The second stage, from the 1920s to the 1960s, is the ascendancy period. The last stage, clearly visible from the 1970s, marks the decline in mine migrancy (Crush et al 1991: 4-12; MacDonald 2000: 13-14). During the formative phase, there was huge demand for labour in the newly opened diamond and gold mines in South Africa. In addition, there was also huge demand for labour both within and outside South Africa. This was partly due to the imposition of colonial taxation and the gruelling lack of better-paying jobs in southern African colonial territories including colonial Malawi.

The South African Chamber of Mines negotiated with a number of countries in southern Africa for labour recruitment from their territories. This culminated in *Wenela* beginning recruitment activities in Malawi in 1903 (Pachai 1973: 119). However, between 1909 and 1934 labour recruitment not only from Malawi, but from most territories to the 'north' was banned due to high death rates amongst black mine workers, especially those from the tropics. The main cause of this high mortality rate were the pulmonary diseases such as tuberculosis and pneumonia (Packard 1989: passim; Chirwa 1992: 124). In Malawi the local planters, who were also looking for local labour, but could not offer competitive wage rates, took advantage of the development to influence the government to ban recruitment (Coleman

3

1972: 38; Paton 1995: 30). Consequently, labour recruitment in Malawi only resumed in 1935.

During the ban years Malawian migrants continued to emigrate to South Africa and Zimbabwe, but on an informal basis (*selufu*). In fact, although formal recruitment was intermittent, for example, during the 1909-1934 ban years and during the world wars because of the war effort, *selufu* continued largely 'undisturbed'. This was in spite of the Nyasaland government efforts to control informal labour migratory flows. After failing to 'control' *selufu*, government switched its focus and merely wanted to 'regulate' it. Paton sheds more light on government's failure to control migration:

> By the 1930s it became clear that prohibition of labour migration was impossible, hence the need to 'control' it. The Lacey Report, a Nyasaland-commissioned enquiry into migrant labour, published a report that was highly critical of the evils of foreign employment. A host of abuses were raised, mainly relating to corrupt recruiters, transporters and employers, and officials who exploited the migrants in various ways. At this time, *matchona* (i.e. those who never returned) were thought to represent 20-30 per cent of all those going abroad. In addition, the standard of living for Africans had fallen abysmally low (Paton 1995: 38).

The government came under pressure from the missionaries and planters to regulate the numbers of people emigrating abroad. Missionaries emphasized the disruptive effects that *selufu* had on the rural areas (Boeder 1974: 198). As for the local planters, they were in favour of reduced numbers of *selufu* migrants since this meant a large pool of local labour at their disposal. What is more, the government itself displayed an ambivalent attitude towards the control of labour migration since, apart from the negative effects highlighted above, increased numbers of emigrants meant increased foreign exchange earnings. In other words, retuning migrants used proceeds to improve the situation within their households and communities. On the whole, this had an overall impact on the measure of development at both local and national levels.

Although *Wenela* started recruiting labour in 1903 in Nyasaland, effective recruitment began in earnest in 1935 after lifting the ban. *Wenela* established recruitment centres across the country: in Mzimba district (northern Malawi), Dowa, Dedza, and Ntcheu (central Malawi), Mangochi and Blantyre (southern Malawi) (see map 1). The distribution of these recruitment centres played a role in determining the nature and form of labour migration from the respective districts. For instance, people in districts with recruitment centres usually emigrated formally i.e. by being engaged by the recruiting agency. Hence in northern Malawi, for instance, the majority of migrants from Mzimba district emigrated under the auspices of *Wenela*, while people from the neighbouring Nkhata-Bay district largely emigrated under *selufu* because there was no recruitment station. A similar pattern developed in central and southern Malawi.

There existed competition between formal migration, in this case *Wenela*, and *selufu*. Each of the two forms of migration had offered its own advantages and disadvantages to the (potential) labour migrants. For example, one of the major attractions of formal migration was the fact that almost everything was provided by the mine management: food, travel and accommodation upon arrival in South Africa. In addition, the Chamber of Mines put in place a deferred payment system, through which part of the migrants' wages were deferred and migrants were accessing their money after the completion of a signed contract. These contracts were usually 9-24 months long. This deferred arrangement ensured that migrants came home with proceeds with which to uplift the financial status and general welfare of their households. However, some disadvantages included the fact that migrants entered a fixed contract and were, therefore, not free to change jobs. The nature of mine work was also tough and dangerous: mines were prone to roofs collapsing, and flooding, among other dangers.

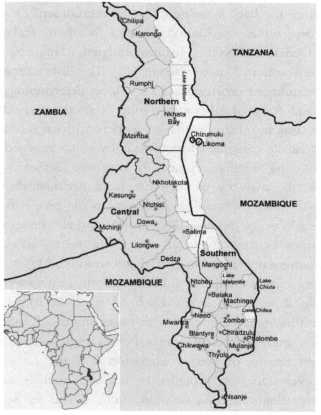

Map 1: Map of Malawi Showing Mzimba (Study District) (Source: ResearchGate)

Selufu, too, offered its own comparative advantages and disadvantages. For example, it was tough for migrants to emigrate under *selufu*: in the old period they used to walk all

6

the way to South Africa, though later they used lorries. But still they met all the transport expenses, themselves. In addition, they had to look for their own accommodation and food upon arrival in South Africa. This was difficult since at times they could stay for a long time without a job. However, the advantage was that they were free to choose jobs and usually changed employers at will, that is, were not bound by a fixed contract arrangement. Even where *selufu* migrants ended up securing wage employment in the mines, the deferred payment system was not applicable, hence they used to get full wages at the end of the month. Consequently, they decided on how to maximize proceeds, for instance, by going for cheaper rented accommodation and food. In short, in addition to the recruitment stations determining the pattern and form of migration, the potential migrants within the districts also decided out of their own volition either to emigrate under *Wenela* or *selufu*.

In 1938 the Rhodesia Native Labour Bureau (RNLB) negotiated with the Nyasaland (Malawi) government to be allowed to recruit labour for the Rhodesian farms. By 1940 the RNLB, which came to be known locally in Malawi as *Mthandizi*,[3] started its recruitment operations. It established recruitment centres in almost the same districts where *Wenela* carried out its recruitment for the South African mines. Consequently, this development ushered in untold competition between *Wenela* and *Mthandizi*. Hence this time competition manifested itself on different fronts (three-pronged): between the external recruiters and local planters and white settlers; between *Wenela* and *selufu*, and, lastly, between *Wenela* and *Mthandizi* (Nkhoma 1995; Banda 2000). In the competition between the latter two, *Wenela* had comparative advantage over *Mthandizi*: the South African mines offered higher wages as compared to the Rhodesian farms, hence more people preferred emigrating under *Wenela*. However, Banda argues, *Mthandizi* too devised her own recruitment strategies and posed a threat to *Wenela*, for instance, by allowing a male migrant to emigrate with his wife and at least one child (Banda 2000). This marked the official beginning of female migration.[4]

In 1936 *Wenela* reached an agreement with the Nyasaland government under which *Wenela* was allowed to resume recruiting for the South African mines. At first the agreement provided for an annual quota of 8,000 recruits on one-year contracts with an option to extend for six months. In 1946 the annual quota was increased to 12,750 and it continued to rise thereafter. By 1973 over 120,000 Malawians were employed on the South African gold mines (Bohning 1981: 30-31). However, just before that, in 1967, *Wenela* reached another agreement with the Malawi government. The 1967 agreement was aimed at increasing employment of Malawians in various sectors of the South African economy. "Whereas after 1963 Africans from Botswana, Lesotho and Swaziland (the popular BLS countries) were relegated to employment in 'specified industries', namely agriculture and mining, in 1967 Malawians were given the opportunity to enter a wide range of occupations" (Bohning 1981: 31).

In the period up to the 1970s the Malawi government encouraged labour migration particularly to South Africa. On this, Paton argues that between 1964 (the year Malawi attained independence from British colonial authorities), and 1967 labour emigration was actually the third largest export in foreign exchange terms after tobacco and tea (Paton 1995: 50). However, the government displayed ambivalence again since, during the same period, "efforts were made to discourage", as it were, "the emigration of the lowest paid (unskilled labour) since they were worth little revenue to the Malawi economy" (Paton 1995: 53). It is noteworthy that immediately after the attainment of independence in 1964 the then President of independent

Malawi, Dr Hastings Kamuzu Banda, encouraged the opening of new estates, especially for tobacco. These estates were eventually opened in the plains of central and northern Malawi. There was, therefore, a huge demand for local labour in these newly-established estates.

In 1974 a plane carrying Malawian *Wenela* migrants crashed in Francistown, Botswana, killing all the 74 miners on board. Dr Banda immediately suspended recruiting and ten days later he decided to withdraw Malawian migrants from the South African mines indefinitely. Most writers have associated the 1974 recruitment ban with the plane crash incident. However, it is important to critically analyse the pre-1974 (ban) labour migration situation from Malawi in order to understand why the ban was imposed in 1974. "Although the 1974 boycott appeared to be sudden, Dr Banda had begun reversing his position on emigration in 1973. He had called on workers to stop going to South Africa, Southern Rhodesia and Tanzania, where he claimed they received low wages compared with the new opportunities for cash-crop profits at home" (Paton 1995: 54). In this case, it might be proper to argue that Dr Banda merely took advantage of the 1974 plane crash incident to officially curtail recruitment and withdraw Malawians from the South African mines. In practice, the boycott was a response to labour shortages on the tobacco estates.

However, the ban was lifted in 1976 following the humble realization that Malawi's feeble economy needed the foreign exchange from jobs abroad. In fact, it is the Malawi government which negotiated with the Chamber of Mines for the resumption of labour recruitment in Malawi. Formal recruiting resumed in Malawi in late 1976 not under the defunct *Wenela*, but under The Employment Bureau of Africa (TEBA),[5] which was popularly known as *Theba*.[6] *Theba* virtually took over the recruitment structures like recruiting stations across the country left by *Wenela*.

9

However, *Theba*, unlike its predecessor, *Wenela*, was looking for smaller numbers of Malawian recruits. This was largely a result of developments within the South African mine industry. The Chamber of Mines had realized that it was incurring huge expenses on foreign recruiting and, coupled with the political and economic instability in those countries, it would be difficult to sustain foreign recruiting. The Chamber, therefore, switched its policy from relying on foreign recruiting to local labour supply. This was made possible by the increase in the price of gold on the international market. This, in turn, enabled the Chamber to increase wages, in the process attracting more black South Africans to work in the mines. This policy of internalization (also called stabilization) went hand in hand with mechanization (Moodie 2001: 5; Wilson 1976: 464).

Since the demand for foreign recruitment amongst Malawians was huge, *Theba* came in with more strict requirements in order to screen the potential recruits. For instance, it deliberately started preferring those applicants with past mine experience: those, who had previously worked under *Wenela*. In this case, such documents as Re-employment Guarantee Certificates (RGCs) (Chirwa 1996: 632-638), Letters of Reference,[7] and Leave Letters facilitated easy re-engagement of potential recruits. Consequently, a good number of former *Wenela* migrants who were not in possession of these documents hardly got engaged by *Theba*.[8] This is partly a reason behind more people opting for *selufu* during the 1980s.

Formal recruitment by *Theba* in Malawi was officially curtailed following the dispute over HIV testing in 1987. South Africa insisted that Malawian recruits were to be tested for HIV before they could be engaged. In response, the government disputed this in line with the World Health Organisation (WHO) principle that all HIV testing should be voluntary (and not compulsory). However, just like the

1974 boycott, there seems to have been other factors behind the 1987 recruitment breakdown. For instance, it has been argued that "with a large South African regional labour surplus, Malawi's expensive fly-in recruits must have seemed expendable to TEBA, especially with Pretoria's pressure (on the Chamber of Mines) to reduce labour dependency on countries other than Botswana, Lesotho and Swaziland" (Paton 1995: 59). Between 1988 and 1992 labour migrants employed in various mines in South Africa were repatriated back home.

With the end of mine migrancy most Malawians who still wanted to go to South Africa emigrated under *selufu*. The majority of repatriated labour migrants were not interested to seek wage employment in the estates and plantations in Malawi because the wages were poor. Consequently, after a brief stay in their villages upon return, they became disillusioned and agitated to go back to South Africa. This time they were ready to look for wage employment in various sectors other than mining. However, it was rather difficult to enter South Africa under *selufu* because of the numerous entry restrictions under the apartheid regime. Nonetheless, it is proper to argue that the decline in mine migrancy led to the increase in the volume of *selufu* migrants from Malawi to South Africa.

Following the collapse of apartheid and the consequent introduction of democratic governance in South Africa in 1994, a number of changes were introduced which favoured the influx of immigrants not only from Malawi, but also other countries such as Zimbabwe and Mozambique. The latter, like Malawi, had always been a major supplier of migrant labour to South Africa. The entry restrictions were lessened and South Africa eventually subscribed to the SADC call for free movement of peoples between countries and trade (economic) liberalization. Similar changes that favoured increased new *selufu* occurred in Malawi: the

11

change in political dispensation from one-party regime to multi-party politics and the improvement in mode of transport between Malawi and South Africa. Following the 'wind of change' that swept across Africa in the early 1990s, the Malawi Congress Party (MCP) regime collapsed in 1994, paving way for democratic governance, just like in South Africa. Thereafter, the political environment favoured the entry of local transporters onto the labour migration scene. A cross-section of Malawians started operating transport business in addition to the established bus companies like Munorurama.[9] These political and socio-economic changes facilitated the entry of more female migrants during the post-1994 period.[10]

2.   Theoretical Framework

This section highlights some of the guiding theories relevant to the issues discussed in the book. In general, the first three theories or approaches are more relevant to the developments during the old labour migration period, especially to formal labour migration or mine migrancy whereas the functional approaches, which focus more on the agency of labour migrants, are relevant to developments both during formal labour migration and *selufu*. What is more, their application tends to cut across both the old and new migration periods. The first three theories in question include the reproduction-centred analysis of labour; the state-centred approach; and the class of African workers approach.

The reproduction-centred approach, which is historically the most influential, focuses on reproductive processes in capitalist societies. There are two versions of this first theory. In the first version, Harold Wolpe argues that "the effects of labour-repressive institutions were to cheapen African labour, and to create and maintain a low-wage labour system" (James 1992: 10). According to Wolpe's analysis, changes in the labour framework could be understood in terms of the changing requirements needed to reproduce low-wage African workers (Wolpe 1972: 425-456). In the case of South African mine industry, migrant labour, mine compounds, and the general lack of trade union representation were all instrumental in reproducing the cheap labour system. The cheap labour power thesis was used to explain the origins and functions of the migrant labour in South African historical studies. The mining companies encouraged a system of migrant labour to avoid maintaining workers' families at the mines, the argument being that because mine work was tough, it was suitable for men (Bozzoli 1983: 143).

A second version of the reproduction-centred approach was advanced by Michael Burawoy in his earlier work on Zambian, South African and Californian migrant labour titled 'The functions and reproduction of migrant labour: Comparative material from Southern Africa and the United States' (Burawoy 1977: 1051-1087). Using a range of comparative material, Burawoy tried to show how an institutionally based conceptualization of migrant labour allowed for a more complex and less economic analysis. A number of limitations of this reproduction-centred approach were highlighted, for instance, that

> Because of its emphasis on reproduction and function, there is a tendency to treat mining capital and the state in an undifferentiated and functionalist manner, and to underplay the divisions between dominant groups. Reproduction analysis can deny individuals and groups an active role in historical processes. It has great difficulty accounting for how subordinate groups attain power, assert interests, and remake institutions. As a result, when applied to South Africa, it pays no attention to African workers in the labour framework:

instead they are reduced to the silent victims of reproductive processes (James 1992: 11).

Secondly, the state-centred approach emerged in response to the shortcomings of the reproduction-centred approach. This approach focused on the active involvement of dominant groups and state officials in the construction of labour-repressive institutions. A notable contribution towards this approach was made by Stanley Greenberg in his book *Race and State in Capitalist Development*. In this book he explored the relationship between labour-repressive state institutions, racial hierarchies and capitalist development in four settings: South Africa, Israel, Northern Ireland and Alabama, United States of America. Greenberg argued that in these societies state officials elaborated and intensified labour-repressive institutions to assist dominant groups in procuring labour during early phases of capitalist development. Other state-centred studies, such as David Yudelman's historical work on the state and the gold mines (Yudelman 1984), have similarly pointed to the centrality of state institutions and state officials in the construction and erosion of labour-repressive institutions. This approach too has its own limitations. Like the reproduction-centred analysis, James argues, "the work on the state pays little attention to African workers" (James 1992: 12).

The third approach was the class power of the African workers approach which arose in the1980s. This approach was to deal with the lacuna or shortfalls of the previous too approaches. By synthesizing labour history and industrial sociology, this approach sought to make sense of the emergence of the independent African trade-union movement in the 1970s and 1980s, the growth of worker power, and the organization of production and labour processes. Though unevenly developed, the literature under this approach sought to document the rise of African workers in the labour framework in the 1980s. however, as Jon Lewis pointed out, "the labour studies literature operated within a narrow frame of reference, rarely going beyond the workplace" (Cited in James 1992: 13).

The other set of theories falls within functionalist approaches. Functional theories focus on the decision-making behaviour (or rationality) of individuals whether to join the migration process or not. The dominant functional theories are neoclassical economics theory (Thieme 2006: 1), the new economics of migration theory (King 2012: 11-12), and human agency theory (Goss and Lindguist 1995: 320). The neoclassical economics theory speculates that international migration is a result of an individual's decision that is taken in the interest of maximizing the migrant's earning potential (King 2012: 12). The new economics of migration theory looks at the household-decision making processes during migration. It maintains that for economically-disadvantaged families, the risk of migrating is too high and this explains why the very poor in origin countries do not tend to migrate. Human agency theory argues that rural producers were not passive victims of their transformation into wage labourers. Instead, they were active participants in the process of *proletarianisation*.[11] One of the advantages of functional theories is their logic and simplicity, for instance, they show that migrants' decisions, whether to migrate or not, are based largely on economic criteria. However, their prediction that competition among migrants would eventually depress wages in the capitalist-rich destination areas may not be evident in some areas (Paton 1973: 6; Goss and Lindguist 1995: 320).

3.   A Note on Methodology

This book is a product of rigorous research that has been conducted over a couple of years using mainly three sources: archival sources, oral sources and secondary sources. This was done to ensure complementarity of sources, bearing in mind that each of these sources has got its own perceived limitations (Vansina 1985: 199). For instance, first, taking the nature of the study into cognizance, archival sources could only be accessed up to the 1980s due to limitations in access policy at the archives and yet the study goes way into the 1990s and beyond. Second, secondary sources proved useful in shedding light on the nature of labour migration history from Malawi to South Africa during the old migration period. This is where a lot of research is concentrated. However, not much substantive research has been conducted, and the findings documented, during the new migrancy period. This is where the significance of this book cannot be over-emphasised. Oral sources proved reliable during the period from the 1970s onwards. This is mainly because in the labour migration areas in Mzimba district I was able to find ex-*Wenela/Theba/selufu* migrants who had fresh memories about their sojourns and experiences in South Africa. The study relied on the use of these oral sources, particularly in the post-1990 period.

Oral interviews were conducted with a cross-section of informants: ex-*Wenela* and ex-*Theba* migrants, ex-*selufu* migrants, current male and female migrants,[12] and key informants. The latter were people with broad knowledge about the history of labour migration from their areas and these included village headmen, primary and secondary school teachers, religious leaders, and herbalists. However, most of these people had not emigrated to, and worked in, South Africa in their lives. The old migrants provided vital information since they were able to shed light on the dynamics of labour migration over time. The study established that although old *selufu* migrants used to face challenges during their stay in South Africa, these challenges

16

pale in the face of numerous challenges faced during the post-1994 period. In order to understand the interface between labour migration and traditional medicinal practices in northern Malawi, oral interviews were also conducted with healers or herbalists based in the labour migration areas. These interviews revealed that these healers play an important role in the migration lives of male and female migrants.[13]

Oral interviews were conducted mainly in the major labour migration areas in Mzimba district. These areas include Zubayumo Makamo area, Manyamula and Engalaweni and villages close to Mzimba district centre (*boma*) in Traditional Authority (T.A.) M'mbelwa; Euthini under T.A. Chindi; and Chasato, Mbwiriwiza and Tchiri under T.A. Kampingo Sibande (all areas) in Mzimba district. Mzimba district was chosen for its continued dominance in labour migration not only in northern Malawi, but in Malawi as a whole. As for archival research, it was conducted over a number of years (1998-1999; 2004-2008; and 2015-2016) at the Malawi National Archives (MNA) main library in Zomba, southern Malawi. Here I consulted various documents under the Historical Manuscripts (in the main library) and Public Archives in the Records Management Centre (section).

4. Structure of the Book

The book contains seven chapters, five of which cover substantive issues on different themes on labour migration from northern Malawi generally, but Mzimba district, in particular. This introductory chapter provides a general overview of the nature of labour migration from northern Malawi to South Africa since the late 19th century. It shows that up to the 1980s migration was either formal (i.e. mine migrancy) or informal (*selufu*). Following the decline of mine migrancy, it became solely informal. The chapter has also highlighted the theories relevant to the emigration of labour both to the mines and other sectors. Among others, in line with the functional theories, the chapter has pointed out that labour migrants are not passive victims of the process of migration, but rather are purposive and rational beings: in view of the potential benefits and 'losses', they decide whether to migrate or not. Lastly, the chapter has highlighted the core methods that were used to collect data that was, in turn, used to develop the chapters in this book.

Although competition in international labour migration manifested itself on several fronts, for example, between formal and informal migration, and between the different recruiting agencies, chapter two examines the competition that 'erupted' between *Wenela* and *Mthandizi* over Malawian labour supply. Having been the first to start its recruitment operations in the country, *Wenela* obviously had an upper hand over *Mthandizi*. However, the study shows, *Mthandizi* proved to be a formidable threat to *Wenela* in some ways. For instance, the strategy to allow male recruits destined for Southern Rhodesian farms to emigrate with their wives attracted a cross-section of potential migrants, including those that had earlier been rejected by *Wenela*. In short, potential labour migrants, who were exposed to both advantages and disadvantages of each of the two recruiting agencies, used their (human) agency and decided through which of the two to emigrate.

In chapter three I examine the joining of female migrants into the labour migration process. The study concentrates on developments in the early 1990s in Zubayumo Makamo area in the western part of Mzimba district. The chapter succinctly argues that although male migrants continued to be dominant in the migration from the district, female labour migrants, in this context minority migrants, became a significant part of the migration process.

Consequently, labour migration stopped being a male preserve, rather it became gendered. The chapter examines both the motivations and decision-making processes behind and during the migration process. On this, it shows that there are minor differences in male and female motivations, but that both male and female labour migrants make either individual or familial (collective) decisions in order to migrate.

In chapter four I focus on the challenges that labour migrants face during their stay in South Africa. Although there are a myriad of these challenges, the chapter focuses on the xenophobic attitudes of the South African nationals towards foreign (migrant) workers. It unveils the kind of suffering that Malawian migrants faced during the xenophobic violence that erupted in May and June in 2008 in South Africa. The paper concludes that the South African hatred against foreigners is rather baseless in that instead of allegations of, for instance, job theft by foreigners, the latter actually contribute towards the economic growth of South Africa.

Chapter five examines developments following the deportation of Malawian migrants from South Africa. It shows that, due to their determination to achieve set goals, *madipotii* (the deportees) easily process their way back to South Africa, hence the concept of recurrent migrants. This is also partly orchestrated by the zeal to avoid societal shame back home where *madipotii* are labelled as *failed migrants*. Most of these migrants face arrests and eventual deportation because their stay in South Africa is illegal following the expiry of their (usual) 30-day visas.

The last substantive chapter (chapter six) examines expressly the linkage between labour migration and the role played by local medicine behind it. This chapter argues that local or traditional medicine plays a crucial role in alleviating the problems that labour migrants face in South Africa. This local medicine, the chapter shows, effectively deals with the challenges in chapters four and five: xenophobic attacks against foreigners and frequent arrests and deportations of illegal immigrants. As a result of the use of local medicine, some labour migrants are able to lead a stress-free life in South Africa. The chapter shows that some of the local medicine (*mankhwala gha chifipa*) were more effective in curing such diseases as sexually transmitted diseases (STDs) unlike Western medicine, hence the popularity of *mankhwala gha chifipa*. The chapter highlights how labour migrants rely on luck medicine and protective medicine in tackling various problems and diseases in South Africa.

References

Banda, H.C.C. (2000) 'Competition for the labour supply in Mzimba District: The case of *Wenela* and *Mthandizi*, 1906-1956', Zomba, Chancellor College, University of Malawi.

Banda, H.C.C. (2008) 'Gendered patterns of Malawian contemporary migrancy: The case of Zubayumo Makamo area in Mzimba district, 1970s-2005' (MA thesis), Zomba, Chancellor College, University of Malawi.

Boeder, R. (1974) *Malawians Abroad: The History of Labour Emigration from Malawi to its Neighbours, 1890 to the Present*, Ann Arbor: East Lansing, Michigan State University.

Bohning, W.R. (ed.) (1981) *Black Migration to South Africa: A Selection of Policy-Oriented Research* Geneva: International Labour Organisation.

Bozzoli, B. 'Marxism, Feminism and South African Studies', *Journal of South African Studies*, 9, 2.

Burawoy, M. (1977) 'The functions and reproduction of migrant labour: Comparative material from Southern

Africa and the United States', *American Journal of Sociology*, 81, 5.

Chirwa, W.C. (1996) 'The Malawi Government and South African Labour Recruiters, 1974-1992', *Journal of Modern African Studies*, 34, 4.

Coleman, G. (1972) 'International labour migration from Malawi, 1875-1966', *Journal of Social Science*, 2, 37.

Crush, J, Jeeves, A and Yudelman, D. (1991) *South Africa's Labour Empire: A History of Black Migrancy to the Gold Mines* Boulder: Westview Press.

Goss, J. and Lindguist, B. (1995) 'Conceptualising International Labour Migration', *International Migration Review*, 29, 2.

Greenberg, S. (1980) *Race and State in Capitalist Development: Comparative Perspectives* New Haven.

James, W.G. (1991) *Our Precious Metal: Labour in South Africa's Gold Industry*, 1970-1990, Cape Town: David Philip Publishers Limited.

King, R. (2012) *Theories and Typologies of Migration: An Overview and a Primer* Malmo: MIM.

Lewis, J. (1990) 'South African Labour History: An Historiographical assessment', *Radical History Review*, 46, 7.

MacDonald, D.A. (ed.) (2000) *On Borders: Perspectives on International Migration in Southern Africa* New York: St. Martin's Press.

Moodie, D.T. with Ndatshe, V. (1994) *Going for Gold: Men, Mines and Migration*, California: California University Press.

Nkhoma, B.G. (1995) 'The Competition for Malawian Labour: Wenela and Mthandizi in Ntcheu, 1935-1956', History Department, Chancellor College, Zomba.

Pachai, B. (1973) *Malawi: The History of the Nation*, London: Longman.

Packard, R. (1989) *White Plague, Black Labour: Tuberculosis and the Political Economy of Health Disease in Africa*, Berkeley: University of California Press.

Paton, B. (1995) *Labour Export Policy in the Development of Southern Africa* Macmillan: Macmillan Press Limited.

Thieme, S. (2006) *Social Networks and Migration: Far West Nepalese Labour Migrants in Delhi*, Munster.

Wilson, F. (1976) 'International Migration in Southern Africa', *International Migration Review*, 10, 4.

Wolpe, H. (1972) 'Capitalism and Cheap Labour Power in South Africa: From Segregation to Apartheid', *Economy and Society*, 1, 4.

Yudelman, D. (1984) *The Emergence of Modern South Africa: State, Capital and the Incorporation of Organised Labour on the South African Gold Fields*, Cape Town: David Philip Publishers Limited.

Vansina, J. (1985) *Oral Tradition as History*, Oxford: James Currey Limited.

Notes

[1] This was in line with the missionaries' view that Africans were uncivilized and backwards, hence needed assistance. To them everything practiced by Africans was bad, and they had to be taught 'the whites' ways', for example, attaining education and converting to Christianity. This was the basis of conflict with Africans who had their own traditional religious beliefs.

[2] *Selufu* is a *Chitumbuka* (one of the local languages) term in northern Malawi coined from the word 'self' as in self-migration or independent migration. The informal migration since the early 1990s is popularly known as new *selufu*.

[3] *Mthandizi* is a *Tumbuka* word in northern Malawi which literally means 'helper'. The RNLB had come to help those people who could not be recruited by *Wenela* emigrate to Southern Rhodesia.

[4] Although *Mthandizi* allowed women to accompany their migrant husbands to Southern Rhodesia (Zimbabwe), female migration to South Africa remained prohibited.

[5] MNA 172/TEBA/1/3/4 WNLA agreement: January 1976-March 1983 (birth of TEBA/ change of company name).

[6] *Theba* was a Chitumbuka and Chichewa (local languages in Malawi) coined from TEBA.

[7] For details on these documents, see Malawi National Archives (MNA) 172/TEBA/1/1/20 Malawi Employees, October 1987; and MNA 172/TEBA/1/1/21 Malawi Employees, October 1987.

[8] Examples of ex-*Wenela* migrants who did not get recruited by *Theba* include Short Nyirenda, Nkhweta Lupunga Village, T.A. chindi, Mzimba, 13/01/2016; Stock Kumwenda, Vuki Village, T.A. Chindi, Mzimba, 13/01/2016; and Kingston Nkhalikali, Vyalema Village, T.A. Chindi, Mzimba, 13/01/2016.

[9] Most of these local transporters were former labour migrants who used part of their proceeds to invest in transport business. They bought pick-up lorries which they used to ply their business between Malawi and South Africa. The pioneers in this kind of transport business were South African nationals.

[10] During the old migration period (i.e. pre-1990 period), women remained at home while their husbands emigrated under *Wenela* and, later, *Theba* to work in South African mines. In the post-1994 women joined the labour migration process initially joining their husbands but later on even as autonomous labour migrants.

[11] *Proletarianisation* in this context is a process whereby rural producers become wage workers or earners.

[12] I interviewed female migrants mainly in Zubayumo Makamo area in Mzimba district as part of my Master's Degree studies at Chancellor College, University of Malawi. I was engaged by Jens Anderson from Holland as a Research Assistant under his research project in Mzimba district and I eventually used part of the proceeds to fund my own research afterwards.

[13] I conducted interviews with healers in 2009 and 2010 together with Markku Hokkanen, a historian from Finland.

Chapter 2

Competition for the Labour Supply in Mzimba District:
The Case of *Wenela* and *Mthandizi*, 1906-1956[1]

1. Introduction

Much of the literature on international labour migration from Malawi to neighbouring countries in southern Africa focuses on such themes as motivations, that is, why people emigrate, the decision-making processes, experiences of migrants and impact of migration. Under motivations, the tendency is to examine the push and pull factors for migration (Banda 2008; Chirwa 1992; Coleman 1973). On decision-making, two central views stand out: first, that labour migration is a result of individual or independent decisions where migrants are seen to migrate without consent from either their guardians (including parents) or partners, in the case of married migrants; second, that labour migration occurs as a result of collective decisions at household level. In the latter case, labour migration is viewed as a family affair whereas in the former case labour migration would be described as a result of rebellion to patriarchal or societal structures. However, few studies touch on the competition that existed between official and clandestine migration, on one hand, and between the labour recruiting agencies, on the other.

This chapter deals with the competition for Malawian labour between the Witwatersrand Native Labour Association, locally known as *Wenela*, and the Rhodesia Native Labour Supply Commission, popularly known as *Mthandizi*.[2] It argues that though *Wenela* was a dominant force in, and was the first to start, the recruitment of Malawian labour, it did not conduct its activities without challenges. It shows that *Mthandizi* posed untold challenges to *Wenela* and at times managed to out-do *Wenela* in the competition. Each of these two recruiting agencies employed strategies that were aimed at attracting and registering more potential migrants than the other. Under such circumstances, the competition between *Wenela* and *Mthandizi* was undoubtedly stiff. However, *Wenela* enjoyed more recruiting advantages over *Mthandizi* in their recruitment operations.

The central argument presented in this chapter is slightly different from the arguments in other local studies on the topic. For instance, a study by B.G. Nkhoma (1995) on the competition between *Wenela* and *Mthandizi* in Ntcheu district has indicated that both *Wenela* and *Mthandizi* stood equal chances of winning the competition, especially after the 1950s. This is in line with studies done elsewhere in the southern African region which have indicated that labour recruiting agencies engaged in fierce competition to attract large numbers of workers.

The chapter also includes the responses of potential Malawian migrants to the job opportunities offered by *Wenela* and *Mthandizi*. On this issue, the chapter argues that with the inception of *Wenela* and *Mthandizi* Malawians were good at exercising their independent choice between *Wenela* and *Mthandizi*. The incentives offered were the determining factors in the people's choice of one recruiting agency against the other. Potential migrants were not passive victims of the circumstances of the time.

The period covered in this chapter is from 1906, when Mzimba District got fully established as part of the colonial state, to 1964,[3] when the colonial period effectively came to an end. This is an important period in Malawian labour migrancy. To begin with, the period covers the years when official migration started in the country to the time it was called off. Official labour recruiting was banned in 1913 and only resumed in 1935. The period also witnessed government attempts to control labour migration – agreements were signed with the external labour recruiting agencies.

The competition between official and independent migration is usually analysed by looking at two crucial periods. The first period is from 1906 to 1936 and the second stretches from 1937 to 1964. The nature of competition during the two periods was different. During the first period competition was not stiff because of the government ban of official recruitment of labour. In support of this, it is argued that during the 1920s there was no large-scale official recruiting of Malawians for work in South Africa and Southern Rhodesia, and, therefore, the migration which took place was mainly independent in nature (Coleman 1973: 40). This implies that independent migration was not affected by government interruption, whereas during the second period independent migration faced competition from official recruiting.

The chapter has five sections. The first section, on methodology, highlights the main sources of information used in the study. It shows that the chapter is based on both oral and written sources in order to advance a balanced view on the nature of the competition between *Wenela* and *Mthandizi*. The second section presents a justification for the choice of the study area. It shows the importance of the study district in as far as labour migration was concerned. Among others, it shows that independent migration played a role in attracting *Wenela* and *Mthandizi* to Mzimba *boma*.[4] The third section focuses on the local factors for emigration. It examines the two contrasting views on the motivations for emigration: tax imposition, on the one hand, and higher wages abroad, on the other. It centrally argues that, on the whole, labour migration was a result of push-pull factors. The fourth section is on the competition between *Wenela* and *Mthandizi*, the main gist of the chapter, presents a critical analysis of the strategies skilfully employed by the two agencies. The last section presents a summary of the conclusions drawn from the chapter.

2. Methodology

The chapter has drawn information from two principal sources: written sources and oral sources. Written sources included both archival sources and secondary literature. The latter comprised books, journal articles, and seminar papers relevant to the study. Most of these yielded valuable information, especially on the nature of labour migration during the study period (Nkhoma 1995: 1-31; Chirwa 1992). Archival information was drawn from the Malawi National Archives (MNA) in Zomba. Archival sources consulted included official information on recruiting organizations, recruiting permits,[5] labour shortages and disputes,[6] identification certificates and official correspondence between Nyasaland Government representatives in Johannesburg and their Nyasaland counterparts regarding conditions of migrant workers.

Oral interviews were conducted with 15 informants and these included ex-migrants (*Wenela* and *Mthandizi*), and potential migrants.[7] Some of these informants had worked with the recruiting agencies, for example, as clerks. All these informants were identified and interviewed in villages around Mzimba *boma*. These informants were identified partly by using snow-ball sampling where an informant identified other ex-*Wenela* and ex-*Mthandizi* migrants in the area. These were then randomly selected based on their availability in the area. It should be noted that a lot of migrants were identified but most of them had emigrated in recent years, that is, in the 1970s and 1980s, hence qualified as ex-TEBA[8] migrants. Despite this, they were very knowledgeable on the nature of the competition between *Wenela* and *Mthandizi.*

3. Mzimba District as a Case Study

The case study of Mzimba district is important for a number of reasons. First, its geographical position: it borders Rumphi district to the north, Kasungu District to the south, Nkhata-Bay district to the east, and Zambia (neighbouring country) to the west. This geographical position was advantageous to labour emigration in a number of ways. For example, the routes taken by migrant labourers from the east cut across the district. Thus the incentives of labour migration from Nkhata-Bay easily reached the intending migrants in the district. Since it is indicated that there was consequent labour emigration from Mzimba, it is conclusive that these incentives were largely attractive. The international border location was favourable to independent migration. Since the latter was not officially allowed by the government, the potential migrants easily sneaked out across the border into Zambia and proceeded south until they reached their respective destinations, either South Africa or Southern Rhodesia (now Zimbabwe). However, it is argued that most migrants had a strong determination to get to the Rand (South Africa), hence so many of them accepted temporary employment in Southern Rhodesia in order to earn enough money to pay for their way to South Africa later on (MNA Recruitment of Labour). It can, therefore, be concluded that most potential migrants had South Africa as their destination.

Second, the people of Mzimba were neighbours of the Tonga of Nkhata-Bay district, who had a long history of participating in labour migration. The Tonga had a migrant tradition. The people of Mzimba were, therefore, influenced by the riches brought home by the Tonga migrants. In fact, most of the Ngoni men used to get employed by Tonga women and were paid out of the proceeds of labour from South Africa and Southern Rhodesia (Kamanga 1997). The people of Mzimba gradually thought of a short cut to prosperity and this was for them to actually emigrate for labour opportunities outside the country and not to be employed in Nkhata-Bay.

The third reason is its economic stand during the period under concern. The people of the district were living in abject poverty, and to add insult to injury, there were very few job opportunities in the district. Among these opportunities was the casual labour on Tonga farms. Under such hardships, the Ngoni were prompted to seek jobs abroad.

Fourth, according to informants, Mzimba acted more or less like the regional headquarters for labour recruitment operations in the north. This necessitates a critical analysis of how the migrants from the neighbouring districts affected the nature of competition between *Wenela* and *Mthandizi* at Mzimba labour market. However, this aspect is not within the scope of this paper.

Finally, the culture of the Ngoni is important in this respect. It is noteworthy that the Ngoni cultural practices encouraged the people to emigrate. The people of Mzimba were of Nguni origin. In fact, their forefathers originated mainly from South Africa and Southern Rhodesia, hence going to these two places for work was more like going back to their roots. What is more, working in these two destinations among fellow Nguni, the migrants were like strangers in their own home.

The two labour recruiting agencies (*Wenela* and *Mthandizi*) knew about the potentiality of Mzimba as a labour source through two principal ways: firstly, through the increasing numbers of independent migrants from the district to South Africa and Southern Rhodesia; and, secondly, through those who had made official contact with the district. In fact, this is more or less the same way by which *Wenela* and *Mthandizi* learned of Ntcheu as a potential labour reserve. However, it is undoubtedly independent migrants who played the most significant role in attracting *Wenela* and *Mthandizi* to Mzimba District. After living with these migrants in South Africa and Southern Rhodesia, employers realized these people were not only trustworthy, but also hard working and were coming in large numbers (Interview Mphande 1999). Consequently, they decided to follow the migrants to their home of origin so as to coordinate the haphazard labour migration.

Most informants were not quite sure about the exact year when *Wenela* came to Mzimba District. Some of them suggested that *Wenela* came to Mzimba in the late 1930s, while others suggested the early 1940s. According to Mr. William Nkhonjera Jere, *Wenela* arrived at Mzimba *boma* in 1938 (Interview Jere 1999). In this paper this is considered as the year when *Wenela* reached Mzimba and it is the year when *Wenela* was re-allowed to start labour recruitment in the country. However, all informants unanimously agreed that *Wenela* came before *Mthandizi*, which arrived in the district after the Second World War. In fact, 1948 is taken as the exact year when *Mthandizi* arrived at Mzimba labour market.

4. Local Factors for Emigration

For there to have been competition either between official and independent migration or between *Wenela* and *Mthandizi*, it means the local people were interested in emigrating and working outside the country. Did the local people start emigrating before or at the arrival of the two labour recruiting agencies? Were the people prompted to emigrate with the presence of the two agencies? Did they already have a migrant tradition? Such questions necessitate a critical review of the reasons why the local people in Mzimba District were willing to emigrate or were actually emigrating. Hence there is need for a critical look at the incentives for emigrating to work abroad and, at the same time, the disincentives to work at home.

There are both conflicting and complementary viewpoints as regards the local factors for emigration. The chapter looks at two such major views. On the one hand, some writers argue that the main motivation for labour migration from Nyasaland (Mzimba inclusive) was the imposition of tax. This view is supported by Coleman (1973: 37) who argues that the imposition and increased rates of tax acted as an incentive for international labour migration from Nyasaland. Local people had to secure money to pay tax and in this connection they had to work for the greatest possible monetary reward. The latter was only possible outside the country, hence emigration. This point is supported by the argument that there were serious disincentives for the people to work for the internal employers in order to secure money for tax. These internal employers preferred to pay the workers in kind rather than in cash and also required labour seasonally. Furthermore, the local people were failing to secure money for tax because of the following factors: the prohibition of sales of cattle after 1910; the lack of cash crop possibilities; and the lack of markets for people's labour.

On the other hand, the second view is against the tax issue and maintains that people emigrated in search for more job opportunities and higher wages. Concurring with this view, Mfune (1982: 2) argues that evidence from northern Mzimba shows that taxation did not play any role in the initial decision of the people to emigrate. He instead argued that the imposition of tax in 1906 and its exorbitant demands only increased the people's desire, which was already there, to emigrate. Mfune's argument is also supported by Sanderson (1961) who argues that the incentive to work for wages, already considerable before the tax was imposed, was further stimulated by a rate of tax that was exceedingly high when compared with the cash earning capacity of the areas. Hence imposition of tax only accelerated labour emigration.

As a counter-argument to both Mfune's and Sanderson's arguments, this chapter is of the view that it would be more appropriate to argue that before the imposition of tax there were reasons for labour migration, one of which was higher wages abroad, and that, later on, the imposition of tax was an additional cause on top of the earlier ones. This chapter slightly disagrees with Mfune when he dismisses tax imposition as not having been a major cause of labour migration. In fact, Mfune uses the verb 'stimulate' which strictly-speaking (in this context) is sort of 'to cause something to happen'. I am of the opinion that the two views are actually complementary. They both imply that the reasons for labour emigration were largely economic, whether the people wanted the money to improve their living standards or to spend part of their proceeds from work on tax settlement. By way of harmonizing the two views, it can be argued that people emigrated because of push-pull factors. The high tax rates, the poor working conditions, the low wages at home were the push factors. On the contrary, the higher wages, and the promising conditions of work abroad were the pull factors – the incentives or attractions for people to emigrate.

Was labour emigration for the uneducated local people only in Mzimba district? On this issue, the Tonga men had a dislike for manual labour at home. "They went abroad, where they were experts of getting skilled or semi-skilled work of a less arduous, and of a more remunerative nature" (Kamanga 1997: 8). From this, it can be concluded that may be the right job for a Tonga with some education was readily available outside the country. On the contrary, educational attainment was portrayed as having been a disincentive for the people to emigrate. In the same vein, Mr. Lackson Chivunga Mphande said that the educated people were not in the habit of migrating either to South Africa or Southern Rhodesia because they were in a position to secure government jobs within the country (Interview Mphande 1999). However, as a counter-argument to the one above, Mr. Abbel Chinisange Shonga quit the teaching profession because of low wages for higher wages in South Africa (Interview Shonga 1999). From the above arguments one can conclude that educational attainment did not necessarily hamper one's inclination to emigrate. What mattered most was job satisfaction as regards wage rates per month, both inside and outside the country.

There were other factors for labour migration. In Mzimba possession of cattle is a mark of wealth and prestige. As a result, people went (and still go) to South Africa and Southern Rhodesia (Zimbabwe) to secure money with which to buy cattle. Related to this cattle accumulation as a causative factor is *malobolo* (bride price). However, Mfune (1982) argues that *malobolo* was not a cause for migration because the bridegroom was not responsible for paying his own *malobolo*, rather this was the duty of his parents and other guardians. The writer of this paper, however, strongly feels *malobolo* was a cause of labour migration, either directly or indirectly. For instance, if one of the family members emigrated to accumulate cattle for *malobolo* of his younger brothers, then *malobolo* here indirectly caused migration, because it is customary for families in the district to find means to buy cattle part of which would solely be used for *malobolo*. Hence to deny the plain fact that *malobolo* was one of the causes of labour migration in Mzimba District would be sheer superficiality.

Another reason for migration was *uswezi* (in Ngoni) or *ukavu* (in Tumbuka), that is, poverty.[9] This is concluded from the observation that most migrants were either married people, those about to marry, or those from poor families. All these categories of people wanted to secure money and material goods with which to support their poor families.

According to informants, the Ngoni of Mzimba, together with the other northern region tribes, already had a migrant tradition. In fact, the reasons for men traditionally migrating to South Africa and Southern Rhodesia become apparent from the women's attitude toward labour migration in the northern region. From personal experience, the writer is of the view that this attitude is directly and wholly applicable to the situation in Mzimba district. Women actually encouraged (and still encourage) their husbands to go abroad for work, as can be seen from the following song by Tumbuka women:

> Banalume balipano ku Harare bakopakochi?
> Balikukoma mzungu?
> Kubaleka ndiko! (Cited in Boeder 1973: 40)

> (Our husbands are around, why don't they go to Harare?
> Did they murder a white person there?
> It's better to divorce them!)

Working in South Africa was (and still is) encouraged because it is regarded as a source of wealth and prestige.

In sum, the competition between *Wenela* and *Mthandizi* was possibly facilitated by the pre-existence of the labour market in Mzimba District. Otherwise it would have been hectic if *Wenela* and *Mthandizi* were to start from scratch —

to implant a migrant tradition in local people. In other words, it would have been difficult to convince them to start emigrating. Since the local people were either already willing to emigrate or were actually emigrating independently, the job of *Wenela* and *Mthandizi* was simplified – they only had to get established, devise recruitment strategies, and start competing for labour.

5. Competition between *Wenela* and *Mthandizi*

Wenela was the first between the two labour recruiting bodies to venture into labour recruiting activities not only in Mzimba District, but also in the entire country. *Wenela* was banned by the government in 1909 and resumed labour recruiting in the country in 1938. From then to the 1950s it established depots in a number of places, some of which were Mzimba, Blantyre and Katumbi (part of Rumphi). During the early years of *Wenela*'s establishment, people came on their own to register with *Wenela* in these places. However, this gradually changed and *Wenela* consequently resorted to active recruiting. Another reason for the change to active recruiting was the competition for labour with the arrival of *Mthandizi* in these places.

Mthandizi, likewise, established recruiting centres in different parts of the country. In fact, the establishment of these centres marked the beginning of active recruiting by *Mthandizi*. Hence it is apparent that at first both these agencies engaged in voluntary or free migration and after the latter proved a failure in providing the employers in South Africa and Southern Rhodesia with the amounts of labour they needed, the two agencies changed to active recruiting (Nkhoma 1995: 13). It was during the latter that competition clearly manifested itself between *Wenela* and *Mthandizi*.

It has been argued that the spirit of competition between *Wenela* and *Mthandizi* was reflected in the way they strategically chose their recruiting centres. Both agencies competed for the same labour supplies and, where their centres were adjacent to each other, it is no surprise at all that they tended to compete.

Wenela was the first to establish centres in most places and *Mthandizi*, later on, introduced centres in almost the same areas where *Wenela* got established. In such a case it is inevitable to conclude that *Mthandizi* was established with the aim of competing with *Wenela*. Again this argument is further strengthened by the realization that soon after arriving at the labour market, *Mthandizi* introduced *ulere*[10] (free) transport system, clearly as a strategy to outbeat *Wenela* in the competition.

In the case of Mzimba District, both *Wenela* and *Mthandizi* established main centres for labour recruitment at Mzimba *boma*. *Mthandizi* followed and established its centre at Davy, close to *Wenela* premises. This signifies the intensity of the competition between the two agencies. It shows that they were competing for the same labour supply. According to Mr. Hezron Gausi (Interview Gausi 1999), although their main recruiting centres were at Mzimba *boma*, the two agencies had periodic market centres in the outlying areas in the district. These were especially places of Traditional Authorities (TAs) and other chiefs, for instance, Mtwalo, Chindi, and M'Mbelwa. *Mthandizi* and *Wenela* officials were visiting such places to publicise their existence at Mzimba *boma*. The local people knew about *Wenela* and *Mthandizi* in the district through such advertisement and publicity. Secondly, they also knew through letters of introduction from *Wenela* and *Mthandizi* through chiefs and local agents who toured the villages. Dates were set beforehand of the periodic markets in different chiefs' centres and when going there the recruiting officials found the people already gathered, ready for registration and transportation to the *boma*.

Although *Wenela* was the first to venture into recruiting, competition between the two implies that each of them had comparative advantages over the other. It is worth noting that the two employed more or less the same strategies, but in order to gain an upper hand in the competition, one of the two agencies had to skilfully employ these incentives, as outlined below.

5.1 *Wenela's* Strategies

Wenela had several advantages over *Mthandizi*: It offered higher wages and more attractive conditions of service; it had created a name on the labour market due to its long recruiting history; it had a bigger catchment area and offered more gifts to its local agents. It also provided free transport (just like *Mthandizi*); free food and accommodation for a longer period; allowances and compensation; and it had more recruiting centres than those of *Mthandizi*. Furthermore, it was better organized and well-funded.

More important is the fact that the employers for whom *Wenela* recruited labourers offered higher wages than almost any other external recruiting agency in the country. Mr. Muzele Mumba supports this argument that *Wenela's* recruits in South Africa were receiving higher wages than *Mthandizi* recruits in Harare (Interview Mumba 1999). In such a case it is not a surprise at all that many people got attracted to *Wenela*. In addition to this, part of the migrants' wages were being given to them on completion of their contracts. This is why these migrants were coming home richer. The riches brought by these returning emigrants were also an incentive for local people to register with *Wenela* and, therefore, against *Mthandizi*. However, it should be noted that the differences in wages were a result of the differences in the nature of the work the labourers were recruited for. *Wenela* recruited for mine work while *Mthandizi* recruited for agricultural work. The latter paid less than the former.

One of the most lucrative strategies employed by the two labour agencies that needs to be critically assessed was the promise of good conditions of service. However, at times these were not adhered to and the impact was damaging on a particular labour agency. In this connection, *Wenela* provided attractive conditions of service to outwit *Mthandizi* in the competition. For example, it gave out wage advances which facilitated clearances of recruits before they started off. Secondly, deferred pay and family remittances were made voluntary. *Wenela* was also good at giving compensation to its recruits (MNA PCN 1/21/25 Workmen's Compensation).

Another advantage for *Wenela* was the establishment of many recruitment centres in the district than those established by *Mthandizi*. Furthermore, informants said that it had a bigger catchment area from where its labourers came. *Mthandizi* recruited only local labour from Mzimba District whereas *Wenela* recruited both local labourers from Mzimba plus those from other districts. This creates the impression that *Wenela* was well known even in the surrounding districts. However, in the actual sense, *Mthandizi* too certainly enjoyed the same advantage, but to a lesser extent, in that it recruited those people from the other districts who were left by *Wenela*.

Another incentive which *Wenela* used in order to attract more recruits was to make sure that its sensitization campaign was much more effective than that of *Mthandizi*. Both agencies aimed at making sure that people in the villages knew of their existence at Mzimba *boma* and they did this through advertisement. They used agents who 'walked all over the place' to publicise their existence. In this exercise the two agencies gave out gifts, for example, blankets for these local agents to take their duties seriously. Both agencies were using more or less the same local agents in the district so much so that these agents campaigned strongly for the agency which was seemingly outstanding in gift-giving. According to Mr. Oswell Sekaseka Hara, *Wenela* used to beat *Mthandizi* on the employment of this strategy (Interview Hara 1999).

Wenela also enjoyed many advantages over *Mthandizi* on the question of provision of free food and accommodation. The latter were provided to registered recruits or those awaiting recruitment and transportation. Informants said that *Wenela* provided these for a longer period than *Mthandizi*. It, therefore, became popular for this. Those who failed to be picked during first recruitment examinations were given second chances, and food and accommodation were provided during the waiting period.

Wenela recruits were supplied with good blankets when starting off for South Africa at Mzimba *boma*, and at Salisbury with suitable clothing before being entrained for South Africa (MNA PCN 1/21/16 Recruiting Organizations). In the same vein, Mr. Hara indicated that *Wenela* was providing clothes inscribed WENELA for identity purposes. This was a status symbol for the *Wenela* recruits. *Bakagubanga munthowa* (they were marching in the streets): Left, Right! Left, Right! He-e *Wenela!* People in the villages got attracted to this. The local people wished they could one day become *Wenela* recruits (Interview Hara 1999).

Free transport was one of the major attractions for people to emigrate officially. Both *Wenela* and *Mthandizi* provided free transport to their recruits. Hence it is safe to say that on transport each of the two agencies enjoyed equal advantages over the other. However, Mr. Million Zimba, a long-time *Wenela* clerk, stressed, arguably, that *Wenela*'s lead in the competition was even manifested in the use of free transport. During each trip on the day of periodic markets three or four *Wenela* lorries were full of registered recruits, unlike *Mthandizi*. However, from a different viewpoint, some records show that *Mthandizi* had a much better transport system than *Wenela*.

Upon realization that *Mthandizi* was a threat after it got established and started its recruiting operations in the district, *Wenela* had to reconsider its strategies as regards their effectiveness by way of reacting to the threat. At times this even involved actually changing some strategies or introducing new ones. For example, *Wenela* changed from free contracting of labour to active recruiting. It also began to offer t-shirts to potential recruits in the villages. Furthermore, it opened air service between Chileka (Malawi) and Francistown (South Africa). This proved to be a big attraction for the local people in Mzimba district.

On the whole, *Wenela*, therefore, seems to have won the competition as regards the numbers procured, especially in the 1950s. This is in line with the views of most of the informants consulted. Available statistical evidence also supports this argument, as can be seen from the table below:

Table 1: Actual number of migrants recruited for South Africa and Southern Rhodesia from 1951-1954

Year	South Africa	Southern Rhodesia
1951	7,828	3,742
1952	6,501	4,654
1953	6,974	6,978
1954	9,844	6,504

Source: Nyasaland Protectorate Annual Reports, 1951-1954. London: HMSO

However, it is worth noting that the above figures do not specify the districts from which the workers were recruited (Chirwa 1992: 395). It is the assumption of this paper that a similar situation obtained in Mzimba district.

5.2 *Mthandizi's* Strategies

Since *Mthandizi* came later in Mzimba district to start recruiting migrant labour, it ended up copying most of the effective strategies employed by *Wenela*. In the first place, *Mthandizi* attracted labourers by its name *Mthandizi* (helper). People got attracted to it, assured of being helped.

Related to the above was the use of attractive recruitment procedures. *Mthandizi* deliberately made its recruitment procedures less rigorous, hence attractive to potential recruits. The latter were not required to undergo a rigorous medical check-up. On the other hand, *Wenela's* procedures were rigorous, with so many stages, hence scared away potential recruits. All people who came were registered by *Mthandizi*. According to informants, this was a strategy by which *Mthandizi* 'equally' managed to recruit a comparatively good number of recruits at Mzimba labour market. According to Mr. Witson Jere, through this strategy *Mthandizi* at one time recruited more recruits than *Wenela* (Interview Jere 1999). However, he could not give the actual figures for comparative purposes. This argument is supported by recruiting figures from written sources and these figures are higher for *Mthandizi*, as can be seen from table 2:

However, the above figures have several weaknesses, for example, they do not include the workers who emigrated without IDs – who were always in large numbers. Furthermore, the figures show the numbers of people who intended to migrate and not who actually emigrated through official channels.

42

Table 2: Issues of Identity Certificates in Nyasaland

Year	South Africa	Southern Rhodesia
1946	7,637	25,650
1947	10,066	23,991
1948	9,936	22,362
1949	8,848	21,981
1950	9,988	20,279

Source: Nyasaland Protectorate Annual Reports, 1946-1953. London: HMSO.

The other strategy employed by *Mthandizi* was the sensitisation campaign. Both *Wenela* and *Mthandizi* used lorries and loud speakers through the village roads publicizing their existence at the *boma*. In this case, those people who lived along roads heard the news directly from the agents. This news gradually got diffused to the 'interior' villages, away from the roads. In this aspect of the competition, *Wenela* was inactive in sensitizing the locals during some years (Interview Ndhlovu 1999), hence *Mthandizi* seemingly took over the lead during such years. However, 'took over the lead during some years' clearly shows it was *Wenela* which was in the lead for a greater part of the six to seven years of their competition, that is, from 1948 to 1956.

It is also indicated that *Mthandizi's* local agents engaged in an intense propaganda campaign for the organization. They were good at intercepting and diverting independent migrants to contract for Southern Rhodesian farms. However, this was also a strategy employed by *Wenela*, and certainly they only differed on the degree to which they pursued this strategy.

In relation to the wages offered by *Wenela*, *Mthandizi* was offering very low wages. This was clearly one of its disincentives. On this, Mr. Gaffar Tembo said: *Ndalama ku*

Mthandizi kukabevye, banthu bakalutirangako suzgo la waka.
(*Mthandizi* was offering low wages, and most people were going there as a last resort) (Interview Tembo 1999). Tembo further stated that *Mthandizi* even closed down its operations towards the end of its operational years in the district partly because of bankruptcy. This shows *Mthandizi* really lacked money and it not a surprise, therefore, that it was giving insufficient money to its recruits.

Contrary to the general consensus that *Wenela*'s working conditions were better than those of *Mthandizi*, Mr. Hezron Gausi argued that it was *Mthandizi*'s working conditions that were better. Gausi had worked as a Public Relations Officer with the Nyasaland Government and at one time he had gone to South African mines on a government mission to see the working conditions in these mines. He discovered and reported that the conditions were bad, contrary to what *Wenela* had been promising during campaign meetings in Mzimba and in Malawi, in general (Interview Gausi 1999). On this argument, I strongly feel that the working conditions in both South African mines and Southern Rhodesian farms kept on changing, and whenever, for example, during certain years working conditions in the mines were bad and potential migrants discovered this, they would be attracted to, and register with, *Mthandizi* against *Wenela*, and vice versa.

Some local people were prompted to register with *Mthandizi* because they were attracted to the nature of jobs they were to perform in the Southern Rhodesian farms. The work was relatively lighter when compared to that offered by *Wenela* in the South African mines. Some people were scared away by *kalavula gaga* (hard labour) in the mines. The lighter work offered by *Mthandizi* is exemplified by the work done by Mr. Lywell Chipanda Nqumayo, a onetime *Mthandizi* recruit. He had been employed to carry out duties like milking cows in the morning only and thereafter he worked in the garden with a lot of leisure time (Interview Nqumayo 1999).

One of the most effective strategies used by *Mthandizi* in the competition was allowing its recruits to go along with their wives. However, it limited the size of the family that went along, for example, a migrant labourer could only go with his wife and one child. Some informants stated that this strategy was adopted after years of *Mthandizi's* recruitment operations, after its realization that it was being outmanoeuvred by *Wenela* in the competition. *Mthandizi* was allowing recruits to go with their wives because of the nature of jobs in the Rhodesian farms. Both male and female labourers could work effectively and efficiently in these farms. For instance, Nqumayo's wife was engaged in seasonal agricultural activities, for example, harvesting maize. Female labourers too were being paid, though relatively lower wages. Consequently, some people got attracted to register with *Mthandizi* because they were allowed to emigrate with their wives and, on top of that, both were being paid, regardless of the differences in their wages (Interview Nqumayo 1999).

Mthandizi also used its already recruited workers working in Southern Rhodesia to recruit their relatives back home on its behalf. These would as well be referred to as having been recruiter-migrants, that is, they were migrants under *Mthandizi*, but were also occasionally playing the role of the recruiter on behalf of their employer. *Mthandizi* provided holidays during which they could come home for such a recruitment exercise. During the latter, *Mthandizi* was providing free transport to and from.

It is worth noting that even songs suggest that the numbers of people *Mthandizi* recruited were large:

Harare ni mukuru, Harare ni mukuru,
nanga ba Nyasaland bangaluta banandi buli

45

kuti wangazula chara (x2) Interview Banda 1999).

(Harare is huge, Harare is huge,
no matter how many Nyasas emigrate there
it will be in a position to accommodate all of them.) (x2)

This song shows the insatiable demand for labour by *Mthandizi*. It also shows that *Mthandizi* too had supporters in the district.

The competition between *Wenela* and *Mthandizi* came to an end in 1956. In that year a strike by *Mthandizi* recruits broke out at Kariba Dam in Southern Rhodesia. The major grievance of the recruits was unfulfilled promises made by *Mthandizi* recruiters in Nyasaland, as R.B. Boeder (1974: 84) observed:

> Reverend Chinula said that the people had been
> attracted to *Mthandizi* because 'it meant help',
> but they did not realize that it actually meant
> 'help the European of Southern Rhodesia'.

The strike resulted in the abolition of labour recruiting in Nyasaland by *Mthandizi* in October 1956. There had been competition for labour at Mzimba market and the withdrawal of *Mthandizi* marked the end of the competition in question. However, *Wenela* continued with its recruitment operations in the district. The withdrawal of *Mthandizi* was followed by the decreasing importance of Southern Rhodesia as a destination for migrant labour and the corresponding growth of South African mines as employers of Malawian labour.

6. Conclusion

The chapter demonstrates that *Wenela* made effective use of the same strategies employed by *Mthandizi* so much so that it ultimately emerged a winner for a greater period of their competition, that is, from 1948 to 1956. It also shows that *Wenela* was better organized, well-funded, and was well known because of its long recruiting history. It is not a surprise, therefore, that *Wenela* emerged a victor in the fierce competition between the rival agencies. However, *Mthandizi* too posed considerable challenges to *Wenela*, for instance, it attracted more people by its name, helper; by the nature of work it offered; and by allowing recruits to go along with their wives. On the whole, the chapter argues that the people exercised their independent choice between *Wenela* and *Mthandizi*.

The chapter also argues that the competition was facilitated by the pre-existence of a migrant tradition among the Ngoni of Mzimba. The people were already willing to emigrate and this was because push-pull factors were at play not only in Mzimba, but in the whole country. The chapter shows that in the case of Mzimba prominent among the push factors were *uswezi* and *malobolo*. Consequently, Mzimba provided a large supply of labour. However, this was also partly because Mzimba acted like a regional market – a catchment area - for the northern region.

References

Secondary Sources

Banda, H.C.C. (2008) 'Gendered Patterns of Malawian Contemporary Migrancy: The Case of

Zubayumo Makamo Area in Mzimba District, 1970s-2005' (Unpublished MA Thesis), Zomba, History Department, Chancellor College, University of Malawi.

Boeder, R.B. (1974) *Malawians Abroad: The History of Labour Emigration from Malawi to its Neighbours, 1890 to the Present*, East Lansing, Michigan: Michigan State University.

Boeder, R.B. (1973) *The Effects of Labour Emigration on Rural Life in Malawi*, Rural Africana:

Michigan State University.

Chirwa, W.C. (1992) '*Theba* is Power: Rural labour, Migrancy and Fishing in Malawi, 1890s to

1985', Kingston: Queens University.

Coleman, G. (1973) 'International Labour Migration from Malawi, 1875-1966'. *Journal of Social*

Science, 2, 37.

Kamanga, E.Y. (1997) 'Labour Immigration and Ngoni labour in Tongaland, 1930s-1960*s*',

History Seminar Paper, Zomba, History Department, Chancellor College, University of Malawi.

Mfune, J.H.C. (1982) 'Labour Migration from Northern Mzimba', History Seminar Paper, Zomba,

History Department, Chancellor College, University of Malawi.

Nkhoma, B.G. (1995) 'The Competition for Malawian Labour: *Wenela* and *Mthandizi* in Ntcheu,

1935-1956', Zomba, History Department, Chancellor College, University of Malawi.

Rubert, S.C. (1991) 'Fresher and ready to Commence Work Without much Delay: The Southern

Rhodesian Ulere Motor Transport System'. Paper presented at the 34th Annual Meeting of African Studies Association, St. Louis. Missouri, Oregon State University.

Sanderson, F.E. (1961) 'The Development of Labour Migration from Nyasaland, 1891-1914'.

Journal of African History, 2, 2.

Van Velsen, J. (1961) 'Labour Migration as a Positive Factor in the Continuity of the Tonga Tribal Society'. In Southall, A. (ed.) *Social change in modern Africa*, London: Oxford University Press.

Primary Sources
Archival Sources

Malawi National Archives (MNA), Recruitment of labour in the Nyasaland Protectorate for

Transvaal and Southern Rhodesia, 1908, 111.

MNA PCN 1/21/25 Workmen's compensation, accidents, requests, 1954-1965.

MNA PCN 1/21/16 Recruiting organizations, 1951-1961.

Oral Interviews

Abbel C. Shonga. Simeon Mvula village. T.A. M'Mbelwa. Mzimba. 18/10/99.

Gaffar Tembo. Kapokolo Kumwenda village. T.A. Kampingo Sibande. Mzimba. 18/10/99.

Harry Chidoba Banda. Londobala Bota village, T.A. Kampingo Sibande. Mzimba 30/10/99.

Hezron L. Gausi, Chinombo village, T.A. Mzikubola, Mzimba, 29/10/99.

Lackson Chivunga Mphande. Mtambalika Moyo village. T.A. M'Mbelwa. Mzimba. 13/10/99.

Lywell C. Nqumayo. Mkhosana Nqumayo village. T.A. Mzikubola. Mzimba. 25/10/99.

Muzele L. Mumba. Chibeta Hara village. T.A. M'Mbelwa. Mzimba. 23/10/99.

Oswell S. Hara. Chibeta Hara village. T.A. M'Mbelwa. Mzimba. 23/10/99.

Pearson Ndhlovu. Mzondi Ndhlovu village. T.A. Mzikubola. Mzimba. 30/10/99.

William N. Jere. Mzondi Ndhlovu village. T.A. Mzikubola. Mzimba. 30/10/99.

Witson Jere. Mzondi Ndhlovu village. T.A. Mzikubola. Mzimba. 29/10/99.

Notes

[1] This chapter is a product of the research work that I conducted as part of my undergraduate studies at Chancellor College, University of Malawi. The findings were first presented at the History Department's seminar in 2000.

[2] *Mthandizi* is a local word for helper. The Rhodesia Native Labour Supply Commission was locally known as *Mthandizi* (helper) because, among other reasons, it was allowing male migrants to emigrate together with their wives. This was not the case with *Wenela*.

[3] Although the paper is looking at the competition between *Wenela* and *Mthandizi* in the period up to 1956, this is a development during the colonial period. In the case of Malawi, this period extended up to 1964.

[4] *Boma* stands for an administrative centre in a colonial district. However, Mzimba nowadays is popularly known as *boma* although there are many such *bomas* in Malawi.

[5] This shows that the recruiting agencies needed permission from the government before they could operate in the country. These permits included quotas, that is, the number of migrants each of them could recruit.

[6] Disputes give an indication of the existence of competition between local employers and external recruiters, on one hand, and between external recruiters themselves, on the other.

[7] Potential migrants were people who were interested in emigrating, but, in some cases, for one reason or another did not make it.

[8] TEBA stands for The Employment Bureau of Africa. This was a recruiting body which replaced *Wenela* after the latter ceased its recruitment operations in the early 1970s. TEBA was locally known as Theba. For details here see Chirwa, W.C. 1992. *Theba is power: Rural labour, migrancy and fishing in Malawi, 1890s-1985*. Kingston: Queens University.

[9] Most of the informants touched on poverty as one of the motivations for labour migration.

[10] *Ulere* is a Tumbuka or Chewa word for free. *Mthandizi* introduced the Southern Rhodesia Free Migrant Labour Transport Services known as *Ulere* in Nyasaland. Through this system, the Southern Rhodesian

government hired lorries to transport self-migrants traveling to Southern Rhodesian farms for free. For details on this free transport system see Rubert, S.C. (1991), 'Fresher and ready to commence work without delay: The Southern Rhodesia *Ulere* transport system', St. Lois. Missouri. Oregon State University. Paper presented at the 34th Annual Meeting of African Studies Association.

Chapter 3

Gendered Migrancy from Mzimba District, Malawi, to South Africa since the 1990s[1]

1. Introduction

In simplistic terms, the history of international labour migration between Malawi and South Africa can be categorized into two periods: the old migration period, 1900s-1970s and the new migration period or contemporary migrancy, since the 1970s (Banda 2008). During the old period, labour migration was largely government-regulated and was facilitated by the labour-recruiting agencies such as *Wenela* and *Mthandizi* (Chirwa 1992; Nkhoma 1995; Banda 2000; Banda 2008). However, a significant proportion of migration during the same period was clandestine in nature and was locally known as *selufu*.[2] During this period, labour migration was almost exclusively a male preserve. From the 1970s onwards, contract migration came to an end and *selufu* escalated.

Much of the literature shows that where women are involved in migration, they are largely involved in commercial aspects of migration, for example, cross-border trade.[3] However, this chapter shows that both men and women from Zubayumo Makamo area emigrate for (unskilled) labour and end up in such sectors as domestic and service sectors.

Using the human agency school, the central argument of the chapter is that despite being a minority in the migration process, female migrants, just like their male counterparts, actively participate in it. This school argues that rural producers are not passive victims of their transformation into wage labourers. Instead, they are active participants in the process of *proletarianisation*, that is, the process of rural dwellers becoming wage workers. For instance, both men and women make either individual or familial decisions in order to emigrate. What is more, both have clear-cut motives which they want to fulfil after a brief period of working in South Africa. However, the chapter reveals that, to a lesser extent, minor differences in motivation between male and female migrants are noticeable. For instance, while both male and female migrants are generally against overstaying in South Africa, a proportion of male migrants, unlike their female counterparts, aim at achieving 'diversification'[4] using proceeds accrued from working in South Africa.

During the contemporary period, labour migration is increasingly becoming feminized as more women, though less relative to male migrants, join the international labour migration scene. In this chapter, gendered migrancy refers to the feminization of international labour migration in which more women are joining the migration process. This chapter aims at examining the form and nature of gendered labour migrancy (i.e. feminization of labour migration from the western part of Mzimba District. The chapter also examines the motives of male and female migrants; the categories involved; and the decision-making processes before migrating. The chapter also aims at showing how the competition between *Wenela* and *Mthandizi* during the old migration period was a factor for the feminization of migrancy.

The chapter is divided into three sections: the research methodology section, which introduces the study area and highlights the methodology employed; the second section examines international labour migration during the old period, that is, during the *Wenela* and *Mthandizi* days. The essence is to show the reasons for the maleness of migration and to establish the beginnings of female migration; the third section is on the gist of the matter, that is, on the feminization of international labour migration from Zubayumo Makamo area.

2. Research Methodology

The evidence for this localized study comes from Zubayumo Makamo area to the west of Mzimba district. The area was chosen firstly because of the perceived existence of female migrancy from the area to South Africa.[5] Secondly, it was chosen because it has a long history of international labour migration and remains one of the major migration areas in the district. In Zubayumo Makamo area there are several 'Makamo' villages. The research findings for this chapter are from five of these villages, viz: Zubayumo Makamo village (proper); Zebediya Makamo village; Kazezani Makamo village; Lithuli Makamo village and Galamala Mgungwe village. All these villages are popularly referred to as Zubayumo Makamo after one of the villages.

The chapter has used three sources: secondary, oral and archival sources. Secondary and archival sources were largely used to provide a historical background of international migration from Malawi and to show the maleness of migration, especially during the old migration period. The information about the study area is mostly from oral sources since there are not enough secondary sources on it.

The following categories of informants were interviewed: male and female migrants; male and female ex-migrants; and male and female potential migrants. Information was collected on their social background, especially childhood and education; the migration histories of their families; the factors for emigration; and the actual emigration process. In addition, key informant interviews were conducted. The interviewees included village headmen, primary school teachers and leaders of different religious institutions. Also interviewed were local businessmen in Zubayumo Makamo area. These included grocery shop-keepers and local transporters.[6]

Unlike the earlier period, the contemporary period is difficult to document statistically because of the informal nature of migrancy. For instance, there are no offices keeping records of male and female migrants. During oral interviews, it was also difficult to compile the numbers of male and female migrants. Informants largely relied on speculating the figures since some of the migrants were away, working in South Africa.[7]

3. Labour Migration during the Old Period

Much of the literature on Malawian migration during the old migration period portrays migrancy as a male phenomenon. The focus of scholars was on general migration issues and not the gendered patterns. This section reflects on some of the literature to show why labour migration was a male preserve. In addition, it advances the argument that female migration started during the same period, for instance, following the competition between *Wenela* and *Mthandizi*.

The cheap labour power thesis was used by most scholars to explain why only men were employed in the mines. It suggested that capitalists introduced migrant labour because it served their interests: "the pre-capitalist sector subsidized the subsistence and reproduction costs of the workers and their households" (Bozzoli 1983; Posel 2004: 1-3). The argument advanced by mine officials was that because mine work was tough, it was, therefore, suitable for men. However, the actual reason was that men

56

were preferred because, once engaged, they were given 'single men's' wages since they left their wives, children and other dependents back home.

During this period, the dominant schools of thought in the literature on labour migration were Modernization and Underdevelopment perspectives (Chirwa 1992: 6-18). Scholars writing from the Modernization Perspective emphasized the positive effects of migration. On the contrary, those writing from the Underdevelopment Perspective advanced the view that labour migration negatively affected the labour source areas. During this period, the emphasis was on general migration issues. Such themes as causes and results of migration featured prominently in the literature.[8] The theme of feminization of migration was largely ignored.

However, it is important to note that women featured in the discussion on the positive and negative effects of migration. For example, on the positive effects, Van Velsen has argued that the Tonga women were transformed into local employers while their migrant husbands were away (Van Velsen 1960: 265-278). This shows an element of rural accumulation and transformation. Kamanga, in expanding van Velsen's argument, shows that these women were using part of the remittances to employ the Ngoni men who used to migrate from Mzimba to Nkhata-Bay for employment (Kamanga 1997).

In order to understand the gendered perspective of labour migration, one needs to look at both *selufu* and contract migration. Both of them show why labour migration was a male preserve. Evidence shows that most people preferred to migrate independently. However, *selufu* was tough and risky. It involved walking on foot for long distances. It also involved taking risks, for instance, braving wild animals and running away from captors on the way to and from South Africa. The following account is an example of the problems that were associated with *selufu*:

> We went to South Africa under *selufu*. We used to walk on foot. I first went to South Africa in 1955. Immediately after we entered the South African border from Botswana we got arrested and we were sent to Bethani, a farm prison, where most of those arrested for illegal entry were sent. There we were forced to dig Irish potatoes using hands. Luckily we managed to escape (Interview Lupafya 2005).

In short, *selufu* was a male domain because of a number of factors. For example, as evident from the above account, men were adventurous and endured hardships in order to secure higher wages abroad. *Selufu* was also a result of the deep-rooted tradition. The society expected men, and not women, to venture out into migration. The Malawi government (called Nyasaland before independence) could hardly control *selufu* because the male migrants were ready to escape even after capture.[9] It is worth noting that this is applicable to *selufu* during the contemporary period. The deportees, popularly known as *madipoti*, are ready to spend a fortune on reprocessing their way back to South Africa and some of them have been deported for a record four times.[10]

Women were not allowed to enter South Africa under contract migration. The recruiting procedure itself was for single men and not for married couples. In the case of *Mthandizi*, women were only allowed later on. The competition between *Wenela* and *Mthandizi* shows how migration was a male preserve in that both agencies were looking for tough men to work in the mines and farms. H.C.C. Banda and B.G. Nkhoma have examined the issue of competition between *Wenela* and *Mthandizi* at length in their works titled *Competition for the labour supply in Mzimba District: The case of Wenela and Mthandizi, 1906-1956*, and *The competition for Malawian labour, Wenela and Mthandizi in Ntcheu District, 1935-1956,* respectively. However, this paper argues that it is the same competition that prompted *Mthandizi* to open up to female migration as a strategy to out-do *Wenela* (Banda 2000).

In addition, it should be noted that the strategies employed by *Wenela* and *Mthandizi* in the competition facilitated the creation of a male identity. For instance, the campaign materials like t-shirts enhanced the maleness of migration. What is more, the agents that *Wenela* and *Mthandizi* engaged, for example chiefs, preferred the emigration of their male subjects.

The other factors that reinforced the male nature of labour migration were the operation of the remittances and the re-employment guarantee system. This was a system whereby migrant workers, for instance, under *Wenela* were given certificates as proof of work experience. During the transition from *Wenela* to TEBA, it was the re-employment guarantee system that enforced the maleness of labour migration. TEBA officials were looking for ex-migrants with mining work experience. Ex-migrants with the Re-employment Guarantee Certificates (MNA 172/TEBA/1/1/20; MNA 172/TEBA/1/1/21; Banda 2008) were easily re-engaged. Evidence shows that the system of remittances reinforced male migration since women remained at home and relied on assistance from their husbands.

There is evidence, though, that despite female migration to South Africa being illegal, some women had interest to go along with male migrants to the extent that some of them managed to enter South Africa clandestinely. The following account supports this view:

While it is appreciated that from humanitarian motives you wish to do your best for our natives, and that Nyasaland natives, both male and female, are able to enter the Union clandestinely, this does not alter the fact that, legally, they are classed as 'prohibited migrants' by the Government of the Union of South Africa... I am, accordingly, to instruct you that you should make it quite clear to applicants that under no circumstances will this government consider issuing passes or facilitating in any way the passage of wives who may wish to join their husbands in the Union (MNA S 36/1/2/6).

The issue of wives accompanying their husbands to South Africa was supported and preferred by some male migrants and female migrants from Zubayumo Makamo area. This is a subject of discussion in the next section.

Human Agency School also shows the decision making processes during the old migration period. For instance, it has been shown that despite *selufu* being tough and dangerous, other people preferred to emigrate through it and not through contract migration. In short, the people were able to weigh the advantages and disadvantages between *selufu* and contract migration before deciding which one of the two to opt for. It has also been shown that despite female migration being illegal in South Africa, some women decided to join their male counterparts, especially under *selufu*.

4. Contemporary Migrancy from Zubayumo Makamo Area

This section examines the nature of labour migration during the contemporary period. As indicated in the research methodology section, it highlights research findings from Zubayumo Makamo area. This section argues that there has been the entry of women into the labour migration system during the contemporary period, hence feminization of labour migration from the area. However, it maintains the view that despite this female entry, male migrants are still dominant, hence the concept of minority labour migrants vis-à-vis female migrants. On the origin of female migration from the area, it was maintained that female migration followed the end of contract migration and the consequent increase in *selufu*.

Until recently, the dominant school in explaining feminization of migration has been the morality thesis. It posits that women were forced out of their home areas into urban areas largely because of the negative impact of male labour migration on the migrants' households. Women are, therefore, portrayed as victims of the male migrant labour system and that, once in urban areas, they resorted to prostitution. Some writers have argued that this view is misleading (Jochelson 1995: 323 332; Gugler 1989: 347-352; Banda 2008). Contrary to the morality thesis, which maintains that women are not decision makers since 'they are forced out by circumstances', these writers have argued that women are not 'passive victims', but 'purposive individuals'. This paper adopts the second view. Using Human Agency Perspectives, this section argues that both male and female migrants are actively involved in decision making to emigrate and that they have clear-cut motives which they want to fulfil by working in South Africa.

On the decision making process, it is important to note that both male and female potential migrants make familial decisions to emigrate. This is in line with the household strategies model, which states that male and female migration follows collective decisions by the family. In this case, male and female migration can be said to be a family affair (Adepoju 2000: 383-394). However, as will be noted later, there are a few cases where potential migrants make individual decisions to emigrate and work in South Africa. Evidence from Zubayumo Makamo area shows that this is

61

common in cases of resistance from the migrants' households. Labour migration in this case is a result of rebellion to familial or household structures.

In addition, it was established that family members agree to send one member, a pioneer migrant, so that he or she would facilitate the eventual emigration of other family members.[11] There were also cases, however, of migrants who emigrated through outright rebellion against, for instance, their parents. Modesta Makamo, daughter of Henry Makamo, is a good example here. The account below was narrated by her father, Henry Makamo, while she was in South Africa, working:

> Modesta got married when she was about to start form two at Mwalawanyenje CDSS in Kasungu District. Her husband was from Ntcheu District. But we, her parents, ended their marriage because the husband was against paying *malobolo* (bride price). Later, we told Modesta to go back to school. But instead she processed her passport without our knowledge. Her sister, Helena, who was already working in South Africa sent her some money, and one day we just discovered Modesta had ran away and joined her sister in South Africa (Interview Makamo 2005).

The above account shows how determined women are to migrate. It shows that they are ready to go against what in the past would have been described as societal or patriarchal expectations: that women would be expected to formally get married and, thereafter, to look after their households. Male migration was regarded as the norm. The situation is fast changing and oral evidence partly shows that some male parents nowadays prefer the emigration of their unmarried daughters at the expense of their sons. The reason given was that it has been discovered that female migrants send more support, for example, in form of remittances back home than their male counterparts.

Feminisation of international migration from Malawi, generally, and from Zubayumo Makamo area, specifically, is a result of several changes that took place both within and outside Malawi in the late 1980s and early 1990s. The following are some of the changes in question: changes in political dispensations both in South Africa and Malawi; changes in the mode of transport between Malawi and South Africa; and, lastly, socio-economic factors (Crush 2000; Chirwa 2001; Matlosa 2001; Banda 2008).

On the changes taking place at the local level, it is worth highlighting the weakening patriarchal control and women empowerment in the area. Evidence shows that weakening patriarchal control came along with 'decentralization' of power not only within the family, but also at the community level. Unlike in the past, women are being empowered through their active involvement in community development projects, for example, church projects. Women are now said to be holding decision making positions.[12] It appears that it is these forms of women empowerment that make women to regard themselves as capable decision makers, just like men. However, it was noted that there are differences among families: some women are becoming more empowered than others (Interview Mwanza 2005).

Unemployment is another factor that pushes women to look for employment away from home. It was indicated that it is extremely difficult to find jobs locally. As a result, emigration is one way for the migrants to earn a living. Sera Mgungwe had this to say on the matter:

I first went to South Africa in 1999 following my husband. I stayed there for two years up to 2001. I was working informally, assisting my husband whenever there was too much work. He was working as a house-keeper. This time my motive is to go and work either at my husband's work place or, if there is no opportunity here, at a distant place. As for this area (Zubayumo Makamo), there are virtually no job opportunities, it being a rural locality (Interview Mgungwe 2005).

Another factor that facilitated the emigration of more men and the joining of women into migrancy is the mode of transport. During the old migration period, migrants, especially under selufu, faced a lot of hurdles on the way to and from South Africa. But during the contemporary period, especially from the 1990s onwards, there have been a lot of improvements in the means of transport. Evidence shows that going to South Africa is nowadays easy because of several coaches and pick-up trucks that transport migrants and their property (*katundu*) between Malawi and South Africa. In Zubayumo Makamo area there are a number of informal transporters that have specialized in this transport business. These transporters were migrants who invested part of their proceeds from their work in South Africa into transport business. These transporters offer favourable conditions to potential male and female migrants. For instance, they transport migrants right to the place of residence of their relatives in South Africa at affordable fares and they sometimes make arrangements to get the money upon arrival in South Africa (Banda 2008).

An example of such local transporters is Anthony Lupafya. He is one of the several migrants from the area who went to South Africa with a view to accumulate enough money with which to set up viable businesses. At the time of the interview, April 2005, he had an iron-roofed house, three tonne pick-up, and a herd of cattle – all these are investments from proceeds from his working in South Africa. This is an instance of labour migrants who have achieved an element of diversification in the area. This is what Anthony said on his initial motive when he went to South Africa:

> We, migrants, differ in our motives. Some do tell the employer (in South Africa) their motive right at the start of the job: 'I will work for one, two or three years and thereafter I will go back home'. But some (the second category) do not do this. That is why they end up overstaying in South Africa. They forget that the wife back home cannot stay for five years without a husband. Hence problems creep in. That is why there marriage break-ups. As for me, I belong to the first category. After a brief stay there I had to come back to stay with my beloved family while doing business (Interview Lupafya 2005).

On the composition of the migrant labour force, different categories of both men and women are involved. It should be noted that male migrants in Zubayumo Makamo area are of all ages: young men; fresh school leavers, including primary school dropouts;[13] middle-aged men; and very old 'ex-official migrants'. The latter are those who emigrated during *Wenela/ Mthandizi* and old *selufu* days, but due to poverty with time they decided to go back during new *selufu* to accumulate some money with which to assist their households.

In the case of women, the dominant categories involved in migration are the wives of migrants, who accompany their husbands; divorcees (Interview Nyirenda 2005);[14] widows, who are left with the burden of looking after their children (Interview Gondwe 2005);[15] and single women, such as, school leavers or unmarried women. The female migrants also differ in their social standing: some are generally poor, while others are better off by village standards. It is the latter category which emigrates with the aim of investing back home, for example, in farming or other businesses.[16] Evidence shows that female migrants, like their male counterparts, have their own respective and genuine motives when emigrating to South Africa.

5. Conclusion

The chapter has shown that while in many places in Malawi international labour migration seems no longer important, it has remained the major strategy to escape poverty in Zubayumo Makamo area. It has examined feminization of labour migration from the area and has shown that this was a result of changes both within and outside Malawi. At the local level, some of these changes include women empowerment and the coming in of local transporters, who are operating their business between Zubayumo Makamo area and the migrants' actual destination right in South Africa. The chapter has argued that during both migration periods labour migration was, and remains, dominated by male migrants. However, it is clear that female migrants, though a minority, are part and parcel of contemporary migrancy, hence the importance of documenting feminization of migrancy. Furthermore, realizing that it is difficult to take one of the two aspects, male or female migrants, out of the picture, the chapter has adopted a gendered approach. Using the human agency perspective, the chapter has succinctly argued that female migrants, like their male counter-parts, are actively involved in emigration and have upright motives which they want to achieve by going to, and working in, South Africa. It has also maintained that international labour migration from Zubayumo Makamo area is largely a family affair.

References

Secondary Sources

Adepoju, A. (2003) 'Continuity and Changing Configurations of Migration to and from the Republic of South Africa', *International Migration*, 41, 1.

Adepoju, A. (2000) 'Issues and Recent Trends in International Migration in Sub-Saharan Africa', *International Social Science Journal*, 165.

Bozzoli, B. (1983) 'Marxism, Feminism and South African Studies', *Journal of South African Studies*, 9, 2.

Banda, H.C.C. (2000) 'Competition for the Labour Supply in Mzimba District: The Case of *Wenela* and *Mthandizi*, 1906 – 1956', Zomba, History Department, Chancellor College, University of Malawi.

Banda, H.C.C. (2008) 'Gendered Patterns of Malawian Contemporary Migrancy: The Case of Zubayumo Makamo Area in Mzimba District, 1970s – 2005' (Unpublished MA Thesis), Zomba, History Department, Chancellor College, University of Malawi.

Chirwa, W.C. (1997) 'No TEBA…forget TEBA: The Plight of Malawian Ex-migrant Workers to South Africa, 1988 – 1994', *International Migration Review*, 31, 3.

Chirwa, W.C. (1992) 'TEBA is power': Rural labour, migrancy and fishing in Malawi, 1890s – 1985' (PhD Thesis) Kingston, Ontario, Queens University.

Chirwa, W.C. (2001) 'The Changing Migration and Employment Patterns in Malawi'. In Matlosa, K. (ed.), *Migration and Development in Southern Africa: Policy Reflections*, Harare: Sapes Trust.

Crush, J. (2000) 'Migrations Past: An historical Overview of Cross-Border Movement in Southern Africa'. In MacDonald, D.A. (ed.), *On Borders: Perspectives on*

International Migration in Southern Africa, New York: St. Martin's Press.

Gugler, J. (1989) 'Women Stay on the Farm No More: Changing Patterns of Rural-Urban Migration in Sub-Saharan Africa', *Journal of Modern African Studies*, 27, 2.

Harawa, L.D. (2009) 'The Impact of Migration on the Socio-Economic Development of Mzimba District: A Case Study of Bulala', Rumphi, Humanities Department, College of Education, University of Livingstonia.

Jochelson, K. (1995) 'Women, Migrancy and Morality: A Problem of Perspective', *Journal of Southern African Studies*, 21, 2.

Kamanga, E.Y. (1997) 'Labour Immigration and Ngoni Labour in Tongaland, 1930-1960s', Seminar Paper, Zomba, History Department, Chancellor College, University of Malawi.

International Labour Office (1998) 'Labour migration to South Africa in the 1990s', Policy Paper Series 4, Southern Africa Multidisciplinary Advisory Team, Harare, Zimbabwe.

Matlosa, K. (2001) 'Overview of Labour Markets and Migration Patterns in Southern Africa'. In Matlosa, K. (ed.), *Migration and Development in Southern Africa: Policy Reflections*, Harare: SAPES Trust.

Mattes, R. et. al. (2000) 'South African Attitudes to Immigrants and Immigration'. In McDonald, D.A. (ed.) *On Borders: Perspectives on International Migration in Southern Africa*, New York: St Martin's Press.

Nkhoma, B.G. (1995) 'The Competition for Malawian Labour: *Wenela* and *Mthandizi* in Ntcheu, 1935 – 1956', Zomba, History Department, Chancellor College, University of Malawi.

Sinclair, M.R. (1998) 'Community, Identity and Gender in Migrant Societies of Southern Africa: Emerging Epistemological Challenges', *International Affairs*, 74, 2.

Taran, P.A. (2000) 'Human Rights of Migrants: Challenges of the New Decade', *International Migration*, 38, 6.

Van Velsen, J. 1960 'Labour Migration as a Positive Factor in the Continuity of Tonga Tribal Society', *Economic Development and Cultural Change*, 8.

Walker, C. (1990) 'Gender and the Development of Migrant Labour System, c. 1850-1930: An Overview'. In Walker, C. (ed.), *Women and Gender in Southern Africa to 1945*, London: James Currey.

Zinyama, L. (2000) 'Who, What, When and Why: Cross-Border Movement from Zimbabwe to South Africa'. In McDonald, D.A. (ed.), *On Borders: Perspectives on International Migration in Southern Africa*, New York: St. Martin's Press.

Primary Sources

Archival Sources

MNA 172/TEBA/1/1/20: Malawi Employees, October 1987

MNA 172/TEBA/1/1/21: Malawi Employees, October 1987

MNA S 36/1/2/6: Female Immigration into South Africa.

Oral Interviews

Anthony Lupafya. Zubayumo Makamo village. T.A. M'Mbelwa. Mzimba. 18/04/2005.

Henry Makamo. Kazezani Makamo village. T.A. M'Mbelwa. Mzimba. 17/04/2005.

Jane Nyirenda. Kapopo Mskanga village. T.A. M'Mbelwa. Mzimba. 16/02/2005.

Lucia Mwanza. Galamala Mgungwe village. T.A. M'Mbelwa. Mzimba. 28/04/2005.

Sera Mgungwe. Galamala Mgungwe village. T.A. M'Mbelwa. Mzimba. 3/05/2005.

Towera Gondwe. Chimbizga Gondwe village. T.A. Chindi, Mzimba. 16/02/2005.

Winstead Lupafya. Zubayumo Makamo village. T/A M'Mbelwa. Mzimba. 17/04/2005.

Notes

[1] The first version of this paper was presented at the international conference on "Histories and National Identities in the Global South: Rethinking the Past and the Present" at Chancellor College, University of Malawi, 12th-15th July 2011. The second version was presented as a history seminar paper at Mzuzu University on 30th May 2014.

[2] *Selufu* is a local term coined from self as in self-migration. Several writers have delved into *selufu*, especially when examining various themes under international migrancy between Malawi and the labour-receiving countries like Zimbabwe (old migration period) and South Africa (both periods).

[3] Cross-border trade (commercial migration) has become an important aspect of migration during contemporary migrancy. Several works have examined it in southern Africa, for example, (1998), 'Labour migration to South Africa in the 1990s'. International Labour Office. Southern Africa Multidisciplinary Advisory Team. Harare. Zimbabwe.

[4] A few male migrants had the express motive of accumulating enough from their 'piece jobs' (*maganyu*) during a brief period, say, three years in South Africa and thereafter coming home to settle, that is, to invest in other endeavours. They were, in short, against regarding working in South Africa as a lifetime occupation. It is from this group of migrants that some ended up becoming transporters and businessmen at Mzimba *boma*.

[5] I first learnt about elements of female migrancy during a visit to the western part of Mzimba District in June 2004. I accompanied Dr. Jens A. Anderson, who eventually conducted research on migrants and transporters in the area later that year. Following this visit, the writer has conducted a lot of research in the area, part of which led to the writer's MA thesis (*Gendered Patterns*). In 2009 and 2010 I also conducted interviews in the area together with Dr. Markku Hokkanen and the

theme this time was labour migration and traditional medicinal beliefs and practices.

[6] It should be noted that there are few grocery shops at Zubayumo Makamo 'trading centre'. This is despite the popularity of migration in the area. It was learnt that migrants use their proceeds in various ways, for example, in farming and businesses like transporting and maize mills. An element of diversification was, therefore, established.

[7] However, estimates were made based on reliable information and in the process the ratio of one female migrant to five male migrants was established.

[8] Most writers focused on general issues such as motives, migration process and impact during the old period. Others examined the nature of migration, for instance, official migration and *selufu*.

[9] Most writers have written on the failure by the Nyasaland (later Malawi) Government to control *selufu*.

[10] The frequent deportations of migrants are another interesting aspect of contemporary migration. Evidence from Zubayumo Makamo area shows that some migrants have prospered after being deported for, say, three times. For details on *madipotii*, see chapter five.

[11] This is common practice in the area. However, it was also learnt that there are rare cases when these pioneer migrants do not deliberately assist their brothers and sisters, sometimes out of sheer jealousy that the younger ones will end up doing better than themselves.

[12] Both male and female informants shared this view.

[13] A good number of male migrants - young and old - indicated they were primary school dropouts.

[14] An example of divorcees (female migrants) is Jane Nyirenda, who divorced her husband in 1988, but went to South Africa in 2000.

[15] An example of widows (female migrants) is Towera Gondwe, whose husband died in 1995, but decided to go to South Africa in 2000.

[16] Most male migrants and non-migrants alluded to the fact that at first people generally thought such female migrants were into promiscuity, but that this thinking has generally changed in the area. They maintained that this is difficult to ascertain and that it also equally applies to male migrants.

Chapter 4

Xenophobic Experiences of Malawian Migrants in South Africa during the Contemporary Migration Period[i]

1. Introduction

The chapter is divided into four sections. The first section attempts to give a contextual definition, if not description, of the term xenophobia. It also valuably examines the historical perspective to xenophobic feelings by South Africans. On this, the chapter advances the argument that xenophobia in South Africa is an old phenomenon, but that it keeps on heightening with an influx of more and more immigrants from South Africa's neighbouring countries. The second section gives a brief overview of the methodology in order to establish the credibility of the research. The third section zeros in on the xenophobic experiences of Malawian migrants, especially during the contemporary migration period. The aim is to allow these migrants to speak for themselves in order to gauge the exact nature of their suffering at the hands of South Africans. It is interesting to note that despite the suffering in question, most Malawian migrants are determined to eke out a living through working in South Africa. Lastly, the chapter highlights worthwhile conclusions drawn from the issues discussed.

Specifically, the chapter examines the experiences of Malawian migrants from the contemporary migration period in southern Africa. During this period most migrants secure jobs in various sectors other than mining. This is a sharp contrast to the period up to the 1970s, the old migration period, when most migrants from Malawi used to work in farms in Zimbabwe and in mines in South Africa. This period can also be referred to as the era of the recruiting agencies (Chirwa 1992; Banda 2000).[ii] It is worth noting that since the early 1990s both men and women, young and old, end up migrating informally to South Africa. Furthermore, while most migrate to secure various jobs, a few of them migrate for trade purposes (Anderson 2004; Banda 2008).[iii]

It is important to briefly outline the methodology employed in the chapter in order to underscore the credibility of the research and its significance in comparison to related research. Some of the information on which this chapter is based comes from the print media following an upsurge of xenophobic violence in South Africa in May 2008. Part of it also comes from the results of the fieldwork among the Malawian ex-migrant workers in June 2004 and April 2005. What are discussed in the subsequent sections are, therefore, the actual experiences of the migrant workers themselves in the face of the trauma in question. Ideally, this approach has been adopted to let the migrants speak for themselves. I also critically reviewed both published and unpublished secondary works on which the primary information, above, is built (Nkhoma 1995; Harawa 2009).

2. Xenophobia: A Definitional Aspect

Since the early 1990s there has been a growing tendency in popular and academic writing to use the term "xenophobia" to explain opposition to immigrants within Southern Africa countries, especially in South Africa. However, most writers do not make efforts to define this term. The conventional dictionary definition of xenophobia is a dislike of foreigners. According to R. Mattes et. al., the etymological roots of xenophobia in South Africa are actually much broader, referring to a "fear of the unknown" or anything that is "different" (Mattes 2000: 210).

This chapter uses this inclusive definition of xenophobia in order to highlight the South Africans' hatred of foreigners, who have different ideas and cultures from theirs. This hatred essentially has to do with stereotypes that South Africans have of foreigners. They view foreigners as a potential threat to their well-being. For instance, the South Africans generally argue that foreigners grab their jobs and contribute to an increase in crime rate.[iv] It is worth noting that the term xenophobia is a complex phenomenon that requires more attention than is usually accorded in the media and academic circles. However, it is not the gist of this paper to examine the term in depth.

Historically, xenophobic feelings among South Africans date as far back as the old migration period (MNA S 36/1/5/5). During this period, there were less such feelings because the process of migration was largely controlled. The recruiting agencies were actually controlling the numbers of able-bodied men who were destined to work in the various designated mines (Boeder 1974; Sanderson 1962: 259-271; Groves 2011; Chirwa 1992). In this case, these migrants were not necessarily a threat since South Africans themselves were shunning mine work. What is more, these migrants occupied the lowest strata of the jobs available in the mines. However, clandestine migrants were ill-treated in various ways by South Africans as the following account illustrates:

The most serious fact I discovered concerns Nyasaland. The WNLA have been stopped recruiting in Nyasaland, but thousands of Nyasaland boys are continuing to make their way on their own to the Transvaal both to farms and mines...and the Nyasaland natives are frequently exploited by touts, ill-treated on farms and are robbed and ruined on the way (MNA S 36/1/5/5).

It is fascinating to note that the situation radically changed towards the late 1980s and early 1990s. This followed the onset of contemporary migration period, since the 1970s, during which migrants went to South Africa informally and ended up securing jobs in various sectors. Research shows that they worked as house keepers, gardeners, cooks, and garage attendants, to mention but some (Banda 2008).

Xenophobia in South Africa can be related to developments in Malawi during the last ten years. In recent years the Government of Malawi has embarked on a crackdown against illegal immigrants from various countries and also refugees who escape from the refugee camps in the country.[v] The notable increase in the numbers of illegal immigrants has in certain respects been matched by a consequent rise of xenophobic feelings among Malawians. They generally view these illegal immigrants as being responsible for the siphoning off of the country's already limited exchange earnings through their prosperous business ventures. In this connection, Felix Manda had this to say: "If you buy items from the shops belonging to *Maburundi*, just know that that is money going down the drain" (Interview Manda 2010).

3. A Historical Perspective of Xenophobia in South Africa

In this section the chapter shows that although xenophobia in South Africa is historically grounded, the experiences of migrants during the old migration period are markedly different from those during the later contemporary period. This is largely due to the fact that during the earlier period, the apartheid era, South Africans and black migrants were both in the same subjective social and economic position – were being victimised by the whites. Following the attainment of independence in 1994, the black South Africans took centre stage and resorted to a blame game – blaming immigrants for their own failure to realise their goals and for all the social ills in society.

Foreign migration is a century-old phenomenon in South Africa. It has been indicated that during the apartheid regime the labour migrants were recruited in droves by employment bureaus from neighbouring countries and exploited. This was unlike the situation of the local unionised workers. Adepoju writes that with political independence in 1994 came a floodgate of mostly illegal migrants who were "eager to partake in Africa's most buoyant economy" (Adepoju 2003: 15). A large number of them brought their skills and enterprise, unlike the largely unskilled agricultural and mine workers of the apartheid era.

In recent years there is a tendency to associate migration and migrants with criminality in South Africa. Foreign migrants (within South Africa) are rapidly coming to be blamed for many of the problems facing South Africans, being linked increasingly to crime, unemployment and lack of service provision. As alluded to earlier, this is the main source of xenophobic feelings by South Africans against immigrants. In this connection, P. Tarran states that "migrants are commonly and deliberately associated with crime, trafficking, drugs, disease and other social ills" (Adepoju 2003: 15). However, available literature shows that there is little evidence that immigrants neither are the cause of the endemic crime situation nor is there concrete proof of a higher crime rate among immigrants than nationals.

In other words, South Africa has become increasingly xenophobic. Unfortunate xenophobic incidents include attacks on hawkers, burning of homes of migrants and inhuman treatment by the police.[vi] Such growing xenophobia stands in jarring contrast to the racial harmony that prevailed during the 1994 election in South Africa.

According to J. Crush, the widespread hostility to immigrants in South Africa can also be explained by the perception that during the apartheid regime the local (black) population held on to the white dominating group as a common enemy. After political independence, the aspirations and expectations of the blacks remained largely unfulfilled. Hence in its place came frustration and disenchantment. In unison, they turn their anger at the immigrants from other African countries accusing them of 'stealing' their jobs, houses and culture (Adepoju 2003: 15). This is largely why immigrants are viewed as a 'force of disruption' rather than as 'vehicles for economic progress'.

On the (new) attitude of South Africans, Sinclair concurs with Crush and writes:

> Long time ago we were never treated like foreigners because everybody, I am referring to blacks, was not allowed to identify himself as an urban resident. South Africans were all entitled to homelands and they regarded us as being better off and since racial segregation was not as harsh as it was in here. This made them to treat us with respect. Again the fact that we were all called "kaffirs" strengthened our bond. Only now that South Africans are allowed to live in towns they have begun ill-treating their fellow brothers (Sinclair 1998: 345).

It can therefore be argued that the South African response to foreigners today is largely one of rejection rather than reception.

It is worth noting that xenophobia in South Africa carries a racial tag. This has been attributed to the effects of the colonial legacy in which everything white is 'pure and good' and everything black is 'bad and evil' (Matlosa 2001: 85). Consequently, immigrants from other continents are viewed as contributors to the country's economic development, whereas Africans (blacks) are viewed with suspicion and as people who take jobs from the local people. This view explains in part the kind of suffering to which immigrants from African countries are subjected while staying in South Africa.

At this point one would be interested to find out as to why employers in South Africa prefer employing foreigners at the expense of South Africans themselves. In the first place, employers find immigrants cheaper to employ. Most of them are categorised as illegal immigrants and, therefore, do not aspire to join unions for fear of being apprehended and deported (MNA PCN 1/21/25; MNA NNM 1/9/1).[vii] Consequently, they fall victim to exploitation by unscrupulous employers, who always threaten to turn them over to the authorities for deportation. The plight of these immigrants working in South Africa is rightly summarised by A. Adepoju who maintains that employers largely describe immigrants as "more skilled, more productive and less militant" (Adepoju 2003: 12).

Immigrants are usually presented as a homogenous category in the literature. What is on the ground, though, is that the so-called illegal immigrants are heterogeneous and include men and women, highly skilled professionals and other informal sector workers who entered South Africa illegally and overstayed as well as those who entered legally but overstayed. These immigrants do all kinds of jobs – both the lowly and highly skilled jobs – that the local population is largely unwilling to do. In so doing, these people go a long way in contributing to the economic progress in the country.

4. Xenophobic Experiences of Migrants *par excellence*

From May 11, 2008, most of the newspapers in Malawi carried articles on the suffering of Malawian migrants staying and working in South Africa. This was a result of the xenophobic attacks by the South African nationals against foreigners. It was reported that the South Africans were irked by low salary offers that immigrants used to jump at. Reportedly, this brought down the salaries that the South African nationals demanded as employers would opt for the immigrants. This is according to 27– year old Felix Naviriyo from Thyolo, 28 – year – old Aida Jafali from Balaka and 24 – year – old Sivati Jalasi from Mangochi (*The Nation* 2008). This view is in line with the view advanced by most Malawian migrants that most poor South Africans accuse African immigrants (in South Africa) of worsening unemployment and perpetrating crime.

It was widely reported in the media that from May 11, 2008 South Africa

> ignored immigrants' right to life and degenerated into ugly scenes, leaving 35, 000 people homeless as armed gangs in the squatter camps and informal settlements in the main urban centres of Johannesburg, Durban and Cape Town went out killing, raping, beating, stabbing and burning nationals from other African countries (*The Nation* 2008).

According to Reuters, mobs armed with knives, stones and in some cases guns began attacking African migrants in Johannesburg shanty town on May 11, 2008. The xenophobic violence later spread to other areas (The Nation 2008).

Following such an outbreak of violence in South Africa, the Government of Malawi took the initiative of repatriating the xenophobic victims back home. Olivia Kumwenda, in an article titled "Government evacuates Malawians from South Africa, first group arrives" (The Nation 2008), indicated that over 100 Malawians arrived in the country on May 25, 2008. According to David Kwanjana, a Malawian immigrant officer who was based in South Africa, the group of repatriated migrants comprised the vulnerable, including the sick, the wounded, mothers, pregnant women and children (The Nation 2008). In fact, this category of migrants was the first to be repatriated. One of the returnees in the group was Ayana Banda, who comes from Thyolo. Ayana with her two children reportedly went to Johannesburg in 2004 following her husband. However, amidst these xenophobic attacks, Ayana's husband opted to remain behind "to gather the little property the family (had) left following an attack on their home" (The Nation 2008).[viii]

Another victim of these violent attacks was Ganizani Chapuma from Thyolo. He was lucky to survive the attack after he was hacked with an axe and left for dead. Chapuma recalled:

> They broke into our house in Ramaphosa, wielding pangas, metal bars, pipes, gallons of petrol and axes, among other weapons, with which they hacked and beat us. They shouted '*ngena*!' demanding that we hurriedly get out of the house. I went out where I was attacked with an axe. They targeted my head and foot. I bled through the ears and was left for dead (The Nation 2008).[ix]

What is worse, their house was set on fire too. Consequently, the fire destroyed all the fortunes he had made in a period of seven months. These included "two bicycles, a television set, a generator, two duvets, three blankets and a car battery" (The Nation 2008). He valued these items at K83, 600.00.

Oral evidence confirms the xenophobic experiences of the Malawian migrants in South Africa. It has been indicated that most migrants from southern African countries generally fail to penetrate other sectors of employment apart from the domestic sector because of xenophobia on the part of South Africans. The latter generally feel that the foreigners worsen the unemployment situation by grabbing jobs from them (Interviews Mzimba 2005). It is worth noting that most of the interviewed migrants in Zubayumo Makamo area in Mzimba district share this view.

In this connection, Trywell Chisi argues that you had to devise mechanisms in order to survive this xenophobia. This is what he had to do:

> Since we were hated, we were forced to change our names. For example, I changed my name from Trywell Chisi to Kingsley Lauhali. You also had to adopt their language as soon as possible. Furthermore, we were forced to marry South African women. In my case, I had a wife here at home, but I married another wife in South Africa so that things should work for me. In fact, even your in-laws, the brothers of your South African wife, would then assist you in securing better jobs. That is why I was able to work in garages and service stations (Interview Chisi 2005).

Trywell Chisi further points out that it was extremely difficult for a foreigner to get promoted at a work place. Consequently, some migrants would even win favours from their bosses through illegal means, for example, through bribery. Chisi sheds light on how, at times, this would be done:

> At times you would be forced to use part of your monthly salary to negotiate with one of the bosses for a

better position during lunch break. After reaching an agreement, you would give him the money. The following day he would shout at you (for no apparent reason): "You fool come here!" And when you come closer, he would tell you that you had been given a better job at such a place (Interview Chisi 2005).

Oral evidence from Chisi, above, and other migrants both at home (Malawi) and abroad (South Africa) shows the desperate and ubiquitous situation of the migrants not only from Malawi, but also from other South Africa's neighbouring countries at the hands of 'militant' South Africans. Such a situation, however, continues unabated.[x]

5. Conclusion

The chapter has succinctly argued that xenophobia in South Africa is historically grounded. It dates back to the old migration days, to the era of the recruiting agencies, when migrants from South Africa's 'satellite countries' were largely working in the mines and farms. Following the attainment of independence in South Africa in 1994, the South Africans became increasingly xenophobic. This was largely because more and more immigrants entered South Africa, some legally while others illegally, to partake in the country's promising economy.

The chapter has also shown that the South Africans' hatred of foreigners is based on fiction and not facts, on unfounded fears that the incomers 'steal' jobs, culture and even women, and that they are a drain on already stretched social services. Contrariwise, these immigrants come with various skills, and are productive and, arguably, contribute to the economic growth of the country.

Towards the end of the chapter, I have dwelt at some length on documenting the xenophobic experiences of migrants during the contemporary migration period. It has been indicated that the Malawian migrants working in South Africa go through traumatic experiences in the face of increasing xenophobia. Such experiences include deaths and loss of property. On this, the chapter advances the argument that the waves of xenophobic violence from May 11, 2008 were unique only in terms of scale or degree, that is, all along migrants had been victims of what may be regarded as salient forms of xenophobia. In this connection, it has been shown that the xenophobic experiences of migrants during the contemporary period are similar to those of the old migrants during the preceding period.

What has not been examined in the chapter is the relationship between xenophobia and the frequent deportations of the illegal migrants in question. It is worth noting that xenophobia has a bearing on these deportations. For instance, it has been indicated in oral sources[xi] that because of the hatred in question, South Africans turn some of these illegal migrants to the police, hence consequent deportations. However, this issue is not necessarily within the scope of this chapter.[xii]

References

Secondary Sources

Adepoju, A. (2003) 'Continuity and Changing Configurations of Migration to and from the Republic of South Africa', *International Migration*, 41, 1, 15.

Anderson, J.A. (2004) 'Informal Migration and Trade in Northern Malawi: Why a Nokia 3310 is

Cheaper in Mzimba than in Johannesburg', History Seminar Paper, Zomba, Chancellor College, University of Malawi.

Banda, H.C.C. (2000) 'Competition for the Labour Supply in Mzimba District: The Case of

Wenela and *Mthandizi*, 1906-1956' (B.Ed Dissertation), Zomba, History Department, Chancellor College, University of Malawi.

Banda, H.C.C. (2008) 'Gendered Patterns of Malawian Contemporary Migrancy: The Case of

Zubayumo Makamo Area in Mzimba District, 1970s-2005' (MA Thesis), Zomba, History Department, Chancellor College, University of Malawi.

Boeder, R.B. (1974) 'Malawians Abroad: The History of Labour Emigration from Malawi to its

Neighbours, 1890 to the Present' (PhD Thesis), Michigan State University.

Chirwa, W.C. (1992) 'TEBA is Power: Rural Labour, Migrancy and Fishing in Malawi, 1890s-

1985' (PhD Thesis), Queens University, Ontario.

Groves, Z. (2011) 'Malawians in Colonial Salisbury: A Social History of Migration in Central

Africa, 1920s-1960s' (PhD Thesis), Keele University.

Harawa, L.D. (2009) 'The Impact of Migration on the Socio-Economic Development of Mzimba

District: A Case Study of Bulala' (B.Ed Dissertation), Rumphi, University of Livingstonia.

Matlosa, K. (ed.) (1998) *Migration and Development in Southern Africa: Policy Reflections*,

Harare: SAPES Trust, 85.

Mattes, R. *et. al.* (2000) 'South African Attitudes to Immigrants and Immigration'. In McDonald,

D.A. (ed.), *On Borders: Perspectives on International Migration in Southern Africa*, New York: St. Martin's Press, 2000, 210.

Nkhoma, B.G. (1995) 'Competition for Malawian Labour: *Wenela* and *Mthandizi* in Ntcheu, 1935-1956' (B.Ed Dissertation). Zomba, History Department, Chancellor College, University of Malawi.

Sanderson, F.E. (1961) 'The Development of Labour Migration from Nyasaland, 1891-1914',
Journal of African History, 11, 2, 259-271.

Sinclair, M.R. (1998) 'Community, Identity and Gender in Migrant Societies in Southern Africa:
Emerging Epistemological Challenges', *International Affairs*, 74, 2, 345.

Archival Sources

Malawi National Archives (MNA) S36/1/5/5 Emigrants: 1941 June – 1947 April.

MNA, PCN 1/21/25: Conditions on the Union of South Africa.

MNA, PCN 1/25/15: Queries from Nyasaland Government Representatives in Johannesburg and Salisbury regarding Migrant Workers: 1951 August – 1960 September.

MNA, NNM 1/9/1 General: 1927 June – 1936 September.

Newspapers

The Nation, 26 May 2008.
The Nation, 28 May 2008.
The Nation, 29 May 2008.

Oral Interviews

Felix Manda, Chibavi Location, Mzuzu, 26/02/2010.

Fletcher Makamo, Zebediya Makamo Village, Mzimba, 15/04/2005.

Genesis Mgungwe, Galamala Mgungwe Village, Mzimba, 30/04/2005.

Gladwell Nthara, Zebediya Makamo Village, Mzimba, 19/04/2005.

Henry Makamo (Interview, Kazezani Makamo Village, Mzimba, 17/04/2005.

Overtoun Lupafya (Interview, Zubayumo Makamo Village, Mzimba, 17/04/2005.

Trywell Chisi, Zebediya Makamo Village, Mzimba, 27 April 2005.

Notes

[i] This chapter initially formed the basis of the paper which was eventually published in the Southern African Peace and Security Studies (SAPSS) Journal in 2013. The paper was titled 'Xenophobia as a Form of Insecurity: The Plight of Malawian Migrants in South Africa' (*Southern African Peace and Security Studies*), 2, 2, 2013.

[ii] The two main competing recruiting agencies in Malawi were the Witwatersrand Native Labour Association (WNLA), locally called *Wenela*, and the Rhodesia Native Labour Bureau (RNLB), locally *Mthandizi*.

[iii] I conducted oral interviews with both migrants and potential migrants in Zubayumo Makamo area in Mzimba District between June 2004 and May 2005. It was revealed that there are three categories of migrants who go to South Africa.

[iv] I conducted a series of interviews with Malawian migrants based in South Africa (Johannesburg, Randburg, among others) in 2005. The results showed clearly the degree of insecurity amongst these migrants. This was a result of not only the hatred and animosity perpetrated by South Africans, but also the fact that most of these migrants were afraid of deportation by the South African police since they usually do not have proper documentation. In other words, they have an illegal status. The same view was echoed by the migrants in Zubayumo Makamo area in Mzimba District.

[v] It was extremely difficult to access official documentation here due to the sensitivity of the matter. Hence lack of statistics in the chapter.

[vi] Such xenophobic attacks will be examined at length in the subsequent section.

[vii] From the interviews I conducted in South Africa, it was clearly evident that these migrants stay in hiding – they are not free to go about in the streets for fear of apprehension.

[viii] This clearly shows the desperate situation in which migrants find themselves in the face of xenophobia in South Africa.

[ix] This is a personal experience of 38-year-old, father of three, Ganizani Chapuma from Thyolo. He went to South Africa's Ramaphosa area where he eventually became a victim of xenophobic violence.

[x] Xenophobic feelings of South Africans against foreigners only changes in scale – at times small-scale, and at other times large-scale. This implies that there are various underlying factors for such a development. However, an examination of such factors is not within the scope of this paper.

[xi] Most informants alluded to the fact that illegal migrants are deported following tips which the police get from South Africans. This is a result of xenophobia.

[xii] See chapter five.

Chapter 5

Madipoti: International Recurrent Migrants from Zubayumo Makamo Area during the Contemporary Migration Period

1. Introduction

International labour migration between Malawi and South Africa dates to as far back as the early 1880s. This labour migration history categorically falls into two periods; the old labour migration period, 1880s - 1970s; and the new labour migration or contemporary period, 1970s to date (Banda 2008). Deportations of 'illegal immigrants'[1] from South Africa can be traced to (as far back as) the old labour migration period. During this period, there were two contrasting categories of labour migrants (here in after migrants): official migrants engaged by labour-recruiting agencies like *Wenela*[2] and *Mthandizi* (Nkhoma 1995; Banda 200); and self or independent migrants (Banda 2000).[3] It was the latter category which was liable for deportations since they were found in South Africa illegally.

During the later contemporary labour migration period, official migration came to an end (Chirwa 1997). However, independent labour migration escalated. This was a result of the fact that more and more migrants including the ex-*Wenela* and ex-*Mthandizi* recruits, continued to migrate informally to South Africa under *selufu*. The chapter argues that this influx of informal migrants did contribute to the ever-increasing number of deported Malawian migrants from South Africa. It is worth noting that these migrants enter South Africa legally, but end up overstaying there, hence illegal migrants. The chapter further argues that most of the deportees, popularly known as *madipoti* (the deported) in Malawi, end up being recurrent migrants because of their determination to go back and accomplish their respective goals. These migrants, as will be noted in the chapter, are usually frustrated for losing their money (Rands), *katundu*, including their hard-worn jobs. They also want to save themselves from shame in their villages since *madipoti* are stereotypically regarded as failed migrants. *Madipoti* are, therefore, ready to spend a fortune, for instance, a lot of money on reprocessing of passports and on transport back to South Africa because of the conviction that what they would eventually accumulate in South Africa would be many times more than this expenditure.

The chapter also shows why some migrants have been deported several times unlike others. Most of the interviewed migrants in Zubayumo Makamo area attribute this to 'carelessness' of the migrants during their stay in South Africa. In order to avoid deportations by the police, they have to remain indoors. However, to a lesser extent, it has been shown that some migrants, though relatively few, effectively avoid deportations in South Africa due to a belief in protective *mankhwala*.[4] This brings in the relationship between labour migration and traditional medicinal beliefs or practices in Mzimba District and in northern Malawi, generally. However, this aspect is not within the scope of this chapter and has, therefore, been dealt with elsewhere.[5]

Since 1994, the end of apartheid in South Africa, there has been growing xenophobia directed at foreigners. This xenophobia has often culminated in physical violence against foreigners themselves or their property. In this connection, xenophobia either directly or indirectly leads to the deportations in question. However, I have already examined this issue in the chapter titled 'Xenophobic

Experiences of Malawian Migrants in South Africa during the Contemporary Migration Period'.[6]

Methodologically, the chapter has taken into account all the three sources; secondary sources, archival sources and oral tradition. The chapter has greatly relied on archival information in order to highlight the kind and nature of deportations of Malawians from South Africa during the old migration period. The chapter focuses on three core issues, viz: definition of concepts; historical perspectives of deportations; and deportations during contemporary migrancy. During the latter the chapter zeroes in on recurrent migration with a view to unveil its impact on the affected households.

2. *Madipoti*: Documented Migrants or Undocumented Migrants?

Migrants fall into several distinct legal and administrative categories. This section examines some of these categories with a view to identify into which category *madipoti* fit. On the one hand, documented migrants would in simple terms be described as temporary residents who are in possession of visitors, business, study or medical permits. However, there is worthwhile evidence that migrants holding legal visitors and business permits work or engage in economic activities once in South Africa.[7]

On the other hand, undocumented migrants are literally-speaking "unauthorised migrants" or "illegal migrants". These are migrants who enter South Africa clandestinely without proper or any documentation, or acquire false papers before or after entry. It is worth noting that "visa overstayers" are also categorised as undocumented migrants who enter South Africa legally, but they purposefully or inadvertently allow their permits to expire and, therefore, become "prohibited persons". In fact, both visa overstayers and unauthorised migrants are categorised as "prohibited persons" under the Aliens Control Act in South Africa (ILO 1998: 11).

Jonathan Crush et al. argue that the category of "undocumented migrants" should be disaggregated into at least three streams: lawful entrants/ unlawful stayers; unlawful entrants/ lawful stayers; and lastly, unlawful entrants/ unlawful stayers. They continue to argue that the "unauthorised" population decreased by over 250, 000 as a result of immigration amnesties between 1996 and 2000 and that the majority of migrants enter South Africa through legal means (Crush et. al. 2005: 12). It can be noted, therefore, that most of the migrants who end up being deported from South Africa fit into the first stream: lawful entrants/ unlawful stayers. They enter South Africa "lawfully" but end up overstaying, especially after securing 'piece jobs'[8] hence unlawful stayers.

At this juncture, it is important to switch to the subject of deportations itself. However, before examining the dimensions of deportations during contemporary migrancy, the chapter will firstly examine the historical perspectives of these deportations, that is, deportations of Malawian migrants from South Africa during the old migration period.

3. Removal, Repatriation and Deportation of Malawian Migrants from South Africa, 1900s – 1970s

Deportation or repatriation of migrants, especially Nyasaland natives,[9] from South Africa is an old phenomenon. As early as the 1930s, Nyasaland migrants working in South Africa were being deported back home for different reasons.[10] In 1936, for instance, the Provincial Commissioner based in Lilongwe wrote the District Commissioners informing them that the Nyasaland natives were being repatriated by the South African Government in batches of 50 (MNA NNM 1/9/1). During contract migration, employers of labour from the labour-sending countries, including Malawi, always had to repatriate contracted workers upon completion of their contract, unless that contract was extended and the extension conformed to legislation regarding maximum length of stay.

Under removals, some migrant workers were banned from entering South Africa for, say, a period of ten years. This is somehow similar to ostracism introduced by Cleisthenes in ancient Greece in order to safeguard the interests of Athenian Democracy. It is fascinating to learn that Cleisthenes himself fell victim of the practice of ostracism. A classic example here is the case of Mr. Musa Jere of Zubayumo Makamo area who reported in 2005 that he had been banned from working in South Africa indefinitely because of illegally having his contract extended. In fact, he said that he was still in possession of his removal certificate together with other South African documents (Interview Jere 2005).

This is what Musa Jere had to say in explaining why he was issued a certificate of removal:

> I went to South Africa under *Wenela* (contract migration) in 1971. In those days it used to be a contract of 18 months. But in my case, realising that my contract was coming to an end (1973), I had it extended since I had befriended the officials so that I stayed there for 2 years. As you know, it was either 18 months or 24 months. I came home in 1973. After I reached Mzimba *boma*, I bribed some officials there. And you know what? I returned to South Africa from Mzimba boma without even reaching home (Zubayumo Makamo).

After I got back to South Africa, that is, to the same mine, I registered for another 18 months. But some officials recognised me that I had gone back unofficially, so I used part of the money I had to bribe them. But upon discovery, my white bosses wrote me a letter of dismissal (certificate of removal) indicating that 'Musa Jere should no longer work in South Africa'. That's how I came back home for good (Interview Jere 2005).

A second example under removal is that of William Ernest Gondwe who was ordered not to return or enter any proclaimed area on the Witwatersrand for a period of ten years. Unfortunately, the reasons for his removal were not indicated in the cited file of the Malawi National Archives (MNA NS 1/13/7).

4. Problems Experienced by Deportees

The aim in this section is to compare and contrast the problems faced by the deportees during the two periods: old and new migration periods. During the old migration period, one of the problems encountered by the deportees along their homeward journey was the unforeseen delays, especially by the means of transport, for example, train. This is evident from the extract of the letter from the Acting Provincial Commissioner to the District Commissioner of Port Herald:

I have the honour to inform you that the Railway Authorities have addressed me on the subject of the delay caused ... by the work of inspecting and listing the batches of native deportees, and in order to endeavour to obviate the difficulty I have to enquire whether it would be possible for you to send a clerk to Sena on Mondays so that he could return on the train with the deportees and prepare the necessary lists before reaching Port Herald (MNA NS 1/13/7).

It is worth noting that the concerned officials were making concerted efforts to lessen such problems, as illustrated by the response of the District Commissioner of Port Herald to the letter above:

With reference to your letter, I have the honour to inform you that I have provisionally arranged with the Traffic Superintendent, Nyasaland Railways, for the train conductor to take down the particulars of the deportees during the journey. This will obviate any such delay as mentioned in your letter (MNA NS 1/13/7).

It was also learnt by the Nyasaland officials that the South African officials were telling repatriates/ deportees that they were being repatriated at the request of the Nyasaland Government. Consequently, the Nyasaland officials were duly advised by the Secretariat in Zomba to deny this allegation. This simply shows that the South African Government had problems justifying the deportations in question.

The other problem faced by the repatriates was that they were being repatriated or deported without allowing them to collect their personal property. This is applicable to the deportation of migrants from South Africa during the contemporary migration period. For details on this, see the case studies of *madipoti* in the subsequent sections.

5. Deportation of Malawian Migrants during Contemporary Migrancy

Under the new labour migrancy, deportations from South Africa are an order of the day. All those migrants who do not have South African IDs[11] and those who have been in South Africa beyond the assigned days are deported back home.[12] The number of Malawian migrants deported from South Africa annually is quite considerable. However, it is relatively small when Malawi is compared with other labour-sending countries in southern Africa, for example, Mozambique and Lesotho. According to G. Kanyenze, of the total 898, 872 deportees (from South Africa) between 1990 and 1997, 82% were from Mozambique, 11% from Zimbabwe, almost 4% from Lesotho, 1% from Swaziland, Malawi and other SADC countries (Kanyenze 2004).

There is a general feeling that South Africa is 'flooded' with illegal aliens. This has given rise to xenophobia. However, some writers have argued that although undocumented migration has undoubtedly increased, the imagery of "floods", "tidal waves", etc. is actually misleading (Crush et al. 2005: 12). This has led to a heated debate on the numbers of undocumented migrants, for instance, in South Africa at each point in time.

The other argument on the issue of deportations is that "undocumented migration", among others, tends to be driven by economic circumstances and in some cases, desperation (Crush et al. 2005: 12). In other words, the point here is that undocumented migration is a rather complicated process, hence policy makers need to address the real issues on the ground, if it is to be controlled. In this connection, K. Matlosa has emphatically argued that "undocumented migration will continuously elude policy makers if they attempt to tighten border security and deport illegal migrants day after another" (Matlosa 2001: 45). In short, deportations of illegal migrants is not necessarily a solution: People still go to South Africa despite the risk of getting deported.

6. Recurrent Migration

Literature shows that the majority of cross-border migrants in southern Africa remain circular migrants. Put differently, although many migrants stay longer than initially intended, their visits are generally seen as temporary. This view is echoed, among other, by D. Posel, who succinctly argues that many migrants who enter South Africa continue to see themselves as circular migrants. They come to South Africa for employment or income-generating opportunities for a definite period and "have very little interest in staying in the country permanently" (Posel 2001: 6). This brings in the concept of recurrent migration where migrants purposefully emigrate to South Africa more than once. Hence circular migrants are in this case recurrent migrants. By going to and working in South Africa more than once, migrants intend to maximize proceeds from migration, yet at the same time remaining in constant touch with their households. Anthony Lupafya had this to say on the matter:

When I was going to South Africa, I did not want to stay there for a long time (i.e. overstaying). I had a clear-cut motive: to accumulate a lot within the shortest time possible and during this period maintain stable relations with my family. Whatever proceeds I was realising from my 'piece jobs' I was investing here at home, for example, buying iron sheets, fertilizer, cattle, etc. After working for a few years, I ventured into transport business and right now I am one of the reputable transporters, transporting migrants and their property between Mzimba District and South Africa (Interview Lupafya 2005).

Similarly, Dickson Sakala could not agree more with Anthony:

In our case, we used to go to South Africa in those old days under *Wenela, Mthandizi* or *selufu*. These days we advise our children not to overstay in South Africa. In my case, I have four sons who are currently working in South Africa. And they are doing fine - investing the proceeds from their work here at home. Consequently, they have built nice iron-roofed houses, have cars and are doing well in agriculture. Its either they come home after a brief stay or it's their wives who follow them, for instance, once a year (Interview Sakala 2005).

However, you may wish to know that there is another dimension of recurrent migration: this is where *madipoti* are compelled to go back to South Africa at whatever cost after having been deported. Due to such deportations, migrants' stay in South Africa, and their work or "piece jobs", to use their preferred term, are curtailed. The implication is that their clear-cut goals cannot be fulfilled. Consequently, filled with the burning desire and determination to accomplish their mission, *madipoti* are ready to re-emigrate using any available means.[13] In short, their deportation is quickly followed by re-emigration which is, inadvertently, followed by yet another deportation and this becomes a cycle, hence recurrent migration. It is this second aspect of recurrent migration which is the main gist of this chapter.

The chapter adopts the case study approach to shed more light on the recurrent migration in question. It is important to pay particular attention to the plight of *madipoti* following deportations and, ultimately, the impact these deportations have on the *madipoti*, specifically, and on their households, generally.

Oral evidence shows that there is consensus among migrants in general and among *madipoti*, specifically, that deportations have a deleterious effect on the accumulation of proceeds and, consequently, on their careers. This is mainly because these deportations always come without notice and they have no time to put their houses in order, for example, leaving their property, including money, in the custody of their colleagues and friends. To make matters worse, they have no time to give notice of leave to their bosses, hence job losses.

Once home, in Malawi, they are actually ridiculed as "failed migrants" and that is why they quickly reprocess their trip back to South Africa. Benjamin Jere has this to say on this:

Right now I want to embark on a project of moulding bricks for sale. I have teamed up with my friends, who also want to go to South Africa. In fact, we were just waiting for the rains to come to an end. Since I was deported, I have always been trying to find means of securing enough money to cater for my expenses on my way back to South Africa, but money is hard to come by here at home. I don't want to stay too long, nonetheless, otherwise it's embarrassing in the eyes of the public. You need to go back as quickly as possible to continue with your mission (Interview Jere 2005).

The question which troubles the *dipoti* is: "why is he or she susceptible to deportations unlike others?" Or put differently and generally, why are some migrants never deported while working in South Africa? This is where traditional medicinal beliefs come in. For instance, oral evidence from Zubayumo Makamo area shows that some migrants believe in use of particular *mankhwala* which effectively protects them from meeting the South Africa police in the streets. Hence the concept *kunogza ulendo* (literary, preparing the trip). This actually requires the potential migrant to adequately prepare for the intended trip, including how he or she is going to ensure a stay without deportations in South Africa. This involves consulting traditional healers or herbalists for *mankhwala gha mwabi* (luck medicine). There are notable herbalists in the area who are specialized in such medicine. Examples of such herbalists include Linesi Mhone and Dickson Sakala (Interview Mhone and Sakala 2010). One of the ex-migrants in the area who believe in protective medicine is Kingston Lupafya. He had worked in South Africa for more than 30 years, but had never been deported (Interview Lupafya 2005).

7. Case Studies: *Madipoti*

Benjamin Jere

Benjamin is a young married man, born in 1982 and is third born in a family of six children. Both parents were still alive at the time of the interview. It is interesting to learn that Benjamin was the first to go to South Africa before his elder brother, Dominic, born in 1979. He took his own initiatives to raise money for the trip, and managed to go to South Africa. While there, he secured some piece jobs, but before long, he got deported back home. He took longer than his friends to go back to South Africa because of financial hardships. However, he was still 'fighting' (trying hard) to go back following the conviction that it is easier to accumulate money in South Africa than back home (Interview Jere 2005).

Just like most labour migrants, Benjamin Jere indicated that he decided to go to South Africa because of problems at home. "Looking at these problems I said 'why don't I go to South Africa to work so as to alleviate the problems (here) at home?'" He said. However, Benjamin indicated that he was unlucky since he only stayed three months in South Africa before he got deported back home. While in South Africa, he maintained that he relied on piece jobs (maganyu), for example, working only three or four days in a week. He kept on changing jobs in the quest of finding a better-paying job. However, one of the challenges he encountered in these jobs was that of commuting since the jobs were at some distance from his place of residence.

Benjamin explained that at the time of their arrest, he was in the company of fellow Malawian migrants, though only one of them was also from his area, Zubayumo Makamo in Mzimba District. However, by the time of the interview in 2005, his friend had already processed his way back to South Africa. Although he was struggling to secure money with which to go back to South Africa, he was still determined to go. He indicated that during the first trip they moulded and sold bricks to raise money for transport and processing a passport and that, together with yet other friends, he was about to embark on a similar brick project:

> For me to find money for transport and for processing my passport, we moulded bricks. There were six of us. After selling the burnt bricks, we shared the money realized. All the six of us went to South Africa. I am the only one back home after being deported; and right now we are about to embark on a similar brick project. Many migrants working in South Africa buy these burnt bricks through their relatives and it is the latter who build houses here at home on their behalf (Interview Jere 2005).

John Jere

John is a clever, young, and married man. He was born in 1978. He dropped out of school in standard five at Mtenthe Primary School in Zubayumo Makamo area. He has been deported for a total of three times. He has experienced a lot of hardships including sickness during his detention just before deportation. He even 'lost' his passport due to credit. Despite all this, he was still making arrangements to go back to South Africa at the time of the interview. He is convinced that he needs to get medicinal assistance (protective medicine) from a herbalist if he is to stay longer in South Africa (Interview Jere 2005).

Unlike Benjamin Jere who had been to South Africa only once, John Jere had been to South Africa for a couple of times. During these trips, he used either pick-ups operated by local transporters or coaches. Like most migrants who rely on migrant relatives, John was welcomed by his in-law, Bright Makamo, upon arrival in South Africa. This in-law greatly assisted him to secure a job before he could stand on his own. John narrated that upon being arrested, migrants are sent to Lindela Repatriation Centre to await their deportation. It is during this waiting period at Lindela that migrants face a lot of challenges. One of the challenges is that they are arrested abruptly and, in most cases, they do not have money with them. Luckily, those with some money are ready to assist those without money. They mainly need this money upon arrival in Malawi to connect transport from the airport to their respective homes:

> We normally assist each other. Some have money while others do not have money. Now those with money do promise to assist those without money upon reaching Blantyre or Lilongwe (Malawi). While in Malawi, they convert the Rands (South Africa currency) to Kwachas (Malawi currency) and assist the friends; and if you have your friends from the same area, it's very easy to assist each other (Interview Jere 2005).

John maintained that this assistance is not in form of credit but that, normally, the one being assisted is obliged to 'pay back' a little something, in one way or another, as a token of appreciation.

John Jere narrated that at one time he fell sick after being arrested and remanded at Lindela, but that because of his determination to fulfil his mission, he immediately went back to South Africa after this ordeal:

> At one time I fell sick while in jail in South Africa. I caught a bad cough and I was purging. I was taken to the hospital. Later on I was deported. I arrived home very weak. I spent a night here at home. The following day I was taken to the hospital, where after getting medication, I got better.

But because I am a man, I did not stay long here before I went back (Interview Jere 2005).

Absalom Makamo

Absalom Makamo is a young man, born in 1974, and got married in 1994 to Mary Ndobera. They have four children together. He is a standard eight primary school drop-out. He was very lucky to get a somewhat permanent job in South Africa in 2000. This was his first trip. However, the unfortunate part of the story is that he got deported twice the same year (Interview Makamo 2005). During his first trip, Absalom indicated that he went to South Africa through his own initiative. He narrated what had actually happened:

> My brother working in South Africa sent me a mountain bike through a transporter. But the bike did not actually reach me. After three months, the transporter told me that it got lost on the way from South Africa. Instead, he gave me K6,000 as reimbursement. It is this money which I used to go to South Africa (Interview Makamo 2005).

Upon arrival in South Africa, Absalom briefly stayed with his elder brother before moving on to stay with his younger father, who was also working in South Africa. However, Absalom was lucky when it comes to securing a job; he only stayed for three days before his father asked his boss for an employment opportunity at his work place. That is how Absalom easily got a job. He was working from Monday to Friday: it was a rather stable job. However, after working for five months, he got arrested and eventually deported. Although he quickly processed his way back to South Africa, he got deported again the same year (2000) and this brought about financial instability in his life such that he had not been able to go back to South Africa during the next four years.

8. Conclusion

A plethora of views and analyses have been advanced on international labour migration, not only between Malawi and South Africa, but in southern Africa in general. This chapter has specifically focused on the case of undocumented migrants vis-à-vis *madipoti* form Zubayumo Makamo area. It has been shown that deportations have a long history in that they can be traced to the old migration period. One of the arguments in the chapter is that *madipoti* during contemporary migrancy share similar experiences with the deportees during the old migration period.

The chapter has advanced the argument that there are two clear-cut aspects of recurrent migration: firstly, where labour migrants voluntarily come home for holiday and go back after a brief stay to continue with their piece jobs; and secondly, recurrent migration due to frequent deportations. On the second aspect, the chapter adopts the case study approach to expose the determination of *madipoti* to go back to South Africa at whatever cost in order to accomplish their mission.

It is worth noting that overstaying and deportations are two sides of the same coin. However, the issue of overstaying has not been examined since it was not directly under the scope of this chapter. A lot that has been written on overstayers *(matchona)* is biased towards the impact of overstaying on the migrants' households.[14] What has not been examined, however, is a succinct account of how some migrants manage to overstay in South Africa where xenophobia is rife and deportations are the order of the day.

References

Adepoju, A. (1983) 'Undocumented Migration in Africa: Trends and Policies', *International Migration*, 26, 2.

Banda, H.C.C. (2000) 'Competition for the Labour Supply in Mzimba District: The Case of *Wenela* and *Mthandizi*, 1906-1956", History Department, Zomba, Chancellor College, University of Malawi.

Banda, H.C.C. (2008) 'Gendered Patterns of Malawian Contemporary Migrancy: The Case of Zubayumo Makamo Area in Mzimba District, 1970s-2005' (Unpublished MA Thesis), History Department, Zomba, Chancellor College, University of Malawi.

Banda, H.C.C. (2010) 'Xenophobic Experiences of Malawian Migrants in South Africa during the Contemporary Migration Period', Unpublished Paper, History Department. Mzuzu University, Mzuzu.

Böhning, W.R. (ed.) (1981) *Black Migration to South Africa: A Selection of Policy-Oriented Research*, Geneva: International Labour Organisation.

Chirwa, W.C. (1998) 'Aliens and Aids in Southern Africa: the Malawi-South Africa Debate', *African Affairs*, 97.

Chirwa, W.C. (1997) 'No TEBA ... Forget TEBA: The Plight of Malawian Ex-migrant Workers to South Africa, 1988-1994', *International Migration Review*, 31, 3.

Chirwa, W.C. (1992) 'TEBA is Power: Rural Labour, Migrancy and Fishing in Malawi, 1890s-1985', PhD Thesis, Queens University, Kingston, Ontario.

Christiansen, R. and Kydd, J. (1983) 'The Return of Malawian Labour from South Africa and Zimbabwe', *Journal of Modern African Studies*, 21.

Crush, J. et al. (2005) 'Migration in Southern Africa'. A Paper Prepared for the Policy Analysis and Research Programme of the Global Commission on International Migration.

De Haan, H. (2000) 'Livelihoods and Poverty: The Role of Migration – A Critical Review of the Migration Literature', *The Journal of Development Studies*, 36.

Human Rights Watch (1998) 'Prohibited Persons: Abuse of Undocumented Migrants, Asylum Seekers, and Refugees in South Africa'.

International Labour Organisation (1998) 'Labour Migration to South Africa in the 1990s', Policy Paper Series, No.4, Southern Africa Multidisciplinary Advisory Team, Harare, Zimbabwe.

Kanyenze, G. (2004) 'African Migrant Labour Situation in Southern Africa'. Paper presented at the ICFTU-AFRO Conference on 'Migrant Labour', Nairobi, 15 -17 March.

Matlosa, K. (ed.) (2001) *Migration and Development in Southern Africa: Policy Reflections*, Harare: SAPES Trust, 2001.

Nkhoma, B.G. (1995) 'The Competition for Malawian Labour: *Wenela* and *Mthandizi* in Ntcheu, 1935-1956', History Department, Zomba, Chancellor College, University of Malawi.

Posel, D. (2004) 'Have Migration Patterns in Post-Apartheid South Africa Changed?' Unpublished Paper.

Primary Sources
Archival Sources

MNA NNM 1/9/1 General: 1927 January – 1936 September.

MNA NS 1/13/7: Repatriates

Oral Interviews

Absalom Makamo, Zubayumo Makamo Village, T.A. M'mbelwa, Mzimba District, 4/05/2005.

Anthony Lupafya, Zubayumo Makamo Village, T.A. M'mbelwa, Mzimba District, 18/04/2005.

Benjamin Jere, Kazezani Makamo Village, T.A. M'mbelwa, Mzimba District, 27/04/2005.

Dickson Sakala, Zubayumo Makamo Village, T.A. M'mbelwa, Mzimba District, 18/04/2005.

John Jere, Kazezani Makamo Village, T.A. M'mbelwa, Mzimba District, 29/04/2005.

Kingston Lupafya, Zubayumo Makamo Village, T.A. M'mbelwa, Mzimba District, 17/04/2005.

Linesi Mhone, Zubayumo Makamo Village, T.A. M'mbelwa, Mzimba District, 20/06/2010.

Musa Jere, Zebediya Makamo Village, T.A. M'Mbelwa, Mzimba District, 4/05/2005.

Notes

[1] The contextual meaning of illegal migrants is an issue of discussion in the subsequent sections of the paper. Effort has also been made to explain other similar or related concepts like undocumented migrants.

[2] *Wenela* and *Mthandizi* were the two notable and official labour-recruiting bodies in Malawi during the old period. *Wenela* is a local name coined from WNLA which stood for Witwatersrand Native Labour Association. *Mthandizi*, which literally means helper, was a local name for RNLB, that is, Rhodesia Native Labour Bureau.

[3] Self-migration was popularly known as *selufu* in northern Malawi. *Selufu* applied to both labour migration periods.

[4] *Mankhwala* is vernacular word (both Tumbuka and Chewa) for medicine. For details on this, see an article by the same writer on the use of traditional medicine by international labour migrants from Zubayumo Makamo area to South Africa.

[5] I have (also) conducted research on these traditional medicinal practices by migrants. It has been learnt that migrants use *mankhwala* for various purposes, for example, for curing diseases and also as 'luck medicine'.

[6] The chapter 'Xenophobic Experiences of Malawian Migrants in South Africa during the Contemporary Migration Period' is on the plight of Malawian labour migrants at the hands of the South Africans.

[7] A few migrants, especially women, reported that they ended up working briefly in South Africa despite the fact that they had gone there

solely to visit their migrant husbands. This is part of the information the writer gathered in the western part of Mzimba District between April and May 2005.

[8] This is a popular term among Malawian migrants either working or seeking work in Johannesburg, Randburg, and other cities in South Africa. Piece jobs are locally known as *maganyu.*

[9] The term native was a derogatory term which was commonly used during the colonial period by whites. The latter were referring to blacks, the indigenous people of a colony, as being inferior, and rather primitive.

[10] One of the reasons for deportation and repatriation during the old period was the end or expiry of a contract e.g. after working for 18 months or two years. Similarly, all those found staying in South Africa without required documents like the South African ID (Identity Card) were deported back to their home countries.

[11] Identity Cards. Migrants and ex-migrants maintained during interviews that it was extremely difficult to acquire these IDs during their migration days. One of the migrants, Fletcher Makamo, actually considered himself a South African citizen because of possessing the South African ID – a very precious document amongst Malawian migrants.

[12] Usually migrants are allocated 30 days to stay in South Africa. Since most of the Malawian migrants go there to seek employment, they stay longer, hence liable for deportations. This view was shared by most migrants in Zubayumo Makamo area.

[13] All the interviewed labour migrants in Zubayumo Makamo area expressed interest to go back to South Africa. In fact, most had already gone back by the time of the interviews. The rest were busy looking for money to facilitate their trips back to South Africa.

[14] Most writers touch on overstaying *(kutchona)* in passing, that is, not as a topic per se. *Kutchona* comes up in the literature on the negative impact of labour migration, stressing that there is negligence of wives and children due to *kutchona.*

Chapter 6

Migrants and Medicines:
The Interface of Migration and Traditional
Medicinal Beliefs in Mzimba District, c. 1940s[1]

1. Introduction

International migration between Malawi and other southern African countries is a century-old phenomenon. It dates to as far back as the 1900s and even before. Compelled by the mandate to pay hut taxes, B. Pachai argues, Malawians worked in industries throughout British southern Africa (Pachai 1973). In short, the history of international labour migration between Malawi and South Africa can be categorized into two periods: the old migration period, 1900s to the 1970s, and the new migration period or contemporary migrancy since the 1970s (Banda 2008)). During the old period, labour migration was largely government-regulated and was facilitated by the labour-recruiting agencies such as the Witwatersrand Native Labour Association (WNLA), locally known as *Wenela* and the Rhodesia Native Labour Bureau (RNLB), locally known as *Mthandizi*, which literally means helper. It is worth noting that *Wenela* was coined from WNLA (Chirwa 1992; Nkhoma 1995; Banda 2000; Banda 2008). However, a significant proportion of migration during the same period was clandestine in nature and was locally known as *selufu*. The latter is a local term coined from 'self' as in self-migration. Several writers have delved into *selufu* (Banda 208; Hokkanen and Banda 2013), especially when examining various themes under international migrancy between

Malawi and the labour-receiving countries like Zimbabwe (old migration period) and South Africa (both periods).

During the contemporary period, literature shows that labour migration is increasingly becoming feminized as more women, though less relative to male migrants, join the international labour migration scene. In fact, it has been maintained that this feminization of international migration is a global trend. Banda has examined at length this aspect of gendered labour migrancy from the western part of Mzimba District in northern Malawi (Banda 2008; MNA S 36/1/2/6). Using human agency theory, he has argued that, though a minority, female migrants actively participate in the labour migration process, just like their male counterparts. Zoe Groves has also studied Malawian migrants in Zimbabwe (then Southern Rhodesia) using a similar approach (Groves 2011).

It is worth noting that during both migration periods and on the international labour migration between Malawi and South Africa, such general issues as motives of migration and impact of migration have been examined in the literature (Boeder 1973; Sanderson 1961: 259-271). However, relatively few studies have examined the linkage between labour migration and medicine. On such studies most scholars have tended to focus on Western medicine vis-à-vis the migrants' health during the labour migration process. However, a few studies have so far examined the linkage between migration and traditional medicinal beliefs and practices *per se*. This chapter zeroes in on this dimension by examining the dynamics of migrancy between northern Malawi (and Mzimba District, in particular) and South Africa.

2. Research Methodology and Guiding Theory

The evidence for this localized study comes from Zubayumo Makamo area to the west of Mzimba District. The area was chosen because it has a long history of international labour migration and remains one of the major labour migration areas in the district. Other labour migration areas in the district are Manyamula, Engalaweni, Chiseng'ezi and Bulala.[2] In Zubayumo Makamo area there are several 'Makamo' villages. The research findings for this chapter are from five of these villages, viz: Zubayumo Makamo village (proper); Zebediya Makamo village; Kazezani Makamo village; Lithuli Makamo village and Galamala Mgungwe village. All these villages are popularly referred to as Zubayumo Makamo after one of the villages in the area.

The chapter has used three sources: secondary, oral and archival sources. Secondary and archival sources were largely used to provide a historical background of international migration from Malawi and to show the maleness of migration, especially during the old migration period. The information about the study area is mostly from oral sources since there are not enough secondary sources on it. The chronological focus of the chapter is from the 1940s when the labour migrants had the opportunity of using both official recruitment channels (*Wenela* and *Mthandizi*) and unofficial means (*selufu*). It is worth noting that official recruitment resumed at the end of the 1930s after having been banned for close to twenty years. Specifically and as this chapter shows, the labour migrants' personal experiences of migration became dominant from the early 1950s and their oral histories span the entire independence period up to the present.

The chapter is informed and guided by functional theories which look at international labour migration as a result of the rationality of the migrants. Examples of such functional theories are human agency theory and the new economics of migration theory. Using human agency theory, the chapter argues that labour migrants and healer-migrants (the latter are migrants who conduct their healing practices while working in South Africa) are rational and purposive individuals. They are determined to achieve their set goals by 'surmounting obstacles' through the use of *mankhwala gha chifipa* (local medicine, but here literally translated as black medicine). The chapter shows that there are different types of *mankhwala gha chifipa* for different purposes; for instance, overcoming deportations and xenophobia; treating various diseases; and securing jobs and gaining favours from employers at the work places. The chapter, therefore, centrally argues that the traditional medicinal beliefs and practices are part and parcel of the survival mechanisms of the Malawian migrants while in South Africa. For instance, it shows that *mankhwala gha mwabi* (luck medicines) play pivotal roles not only in job seeking, but also in the migrants' 'safety'. In this case, this study aims at complementing the existing historical scholarship on migration and medicine by focusing on Malawian migrants in transit and at their destination, that is, South Africa.

The chapter further argues that most of the deportees, popularly known as *madipotii* (the deported) in Malawi, end up being recurrent migrants because of their determination to go back and accomplish their respective goals. These migrants, as will be noted in the chapter, are usually frustrated for losing their money (Rands), *katundu*, including their hard-worn jobs. They also want to save themselves from shame in their villages since *madipotii* are stereotypically regarded as failed migrants. *Madipotii* are, therefore, ready to spend a fortune, for instance, a lot of money on reprocessing of passports and on transport back to South Africa because of the conviction that what they would eventually accumulate in South Africa would be many times more than this expenditure.

The chapter also shows why some migrants have been deported several times unlike others. Most of the interviewed migrants in Zubayumo Makamo area attribute this to 'carelessness' of the migrants during their stay in South Africa. In order to avoid deportations by the police, they have to remain indoors. However, to a lesser extent, it has been shown that some migrants, though relatively few, effectively avoid deportations in South Africa due to a belief in protective *mankhwala* (medicine). This brings in the relationship between labour migration and traditional medicinal beliefs or practices in Mzimba District and in northern Malawi, generally.

3. Male Labour Recruitment, *Selufu* and Migrants' Health

Much of the literature on Malawian migration during the old migration period portrays migrancy as a male phenomenon. The focus was on general migration issues and not gendered patterns. The cheap labour power thesis was used by most scholars to explain why only men were employed in the mines. It suggested that capitalists introduced migrant labour because it served their interests: "the pre-capitalist sector subsidized the subsistence and reproduction costs of the workers and their households" (Bozzoli 1983; Posel 2004: 1-3). The argument advanced by mine officials was that because mine work was tough, it was, therefore, suitable for men. However, the actual reason was that men were preferred because, once engaged, they were given 'single men's' wages since they left their wives, children and other dependents back home.

In order to understand the ungendered perspective of labour migration, one needs to look at both *selufu* and contract migration. Both of them show why labour migration was a male preserve. Evidence shows that most people preferred to migrate independently. However, *selufu* was tough and risky. It involved walking on foot for long distances. It also involved taking risks, for instance, braving wild animals and running away from captors on the way to and from South Africa. The following account is an example of the problems that were associated with *selufu*:

We went to South Africa under *selufu*. We used to walk on foot. I first went to South Africa in 1955. Immediately after we entered the South African border from Botswana we got arrested and we were sent to Bethani, a farm prison, where most of those arrested for illegal entry were sent. There we were forced to dig Irish potatoes using hands. Luckily we managed to escape (Interview Lupafya 2005).

In short, *selufu* was a male domain because of a number of factors. For example, as evident from the above account, men were adventurous and endured hardships in order to secure higher wages abroad. *Selufu* was also a result of the deep-rooted tradition. The society expected men, and not women, to venture out into migration. The government could hardly control *selufu* because the male migrants were ready to escape even after capture.[3] It is fascinating to note that this is applicable to *selufu* during the contemporary period. *Madipotii* are ready to spend a fortune on reprocessing their way back to South Africa and some of them have been deported for a record four times.[4]

The rapid expansion of the mining industry from the end of the 19th century up to the First World War, Randall Packard argues, caused the demand of labour on all mines to exceed the available supply (Packard 1989: 68). This labour shortage was produced by African resistance to low wages and to the unhealthy, life-threatening living and working conditions on the mines. In order to acquire an adequate supply of African workers, mine owners employed a number of recruiting agencies, contractors and touts to round up potential workers. Intense competition among the mining companies at times led to the recruitment of workers who were unfit to cope with the physical conditions of mine life. Consequently, such workers usually succumbed to diseases, including TB, especially during the first months of their contracts.

The stiff competition between the recruiting agencies (*Wenela* and *Mthandizi* in the case of Malawi) also shows how desperate potential migrants were to ensure that they were engaged. Most potential migrants were destined to South Africa because of the attraction of higher wages as compared to Southern Rhodesia (Zimbabwe). Since *Wenela* was looking for healthy young men, all those who were sickly and underweight were left out during the recruitment process. Oral evidence shows that it is this category of potential migrants who resorted to the use of local medicine in order to increase their chances of being recruited by either *Wenela* or *Mthandizi*, as can be illustrated by the following account:

> With *Wenela* and *Mthandizi*, they were weighing potential migrants. If some people weighed less, they could be given food for two weeks to increase their weight. As a result there were some who could use local medicine to make sure they successfully went through this medical examination. However, it is worth noting that such medicine was bordering on *masalamusi* or *masenga* (use of bad medicine related to witchcraft) (Interview Sakala 2010).

The competition between *Wenela* and *Mthandizi* also shows how migration was a male preserve in that both agencies were looking for tough men to work in the mines and farms. H.C.C. Banda and B.G. Nkhoma have examined the issue of competition between *Wenela* and *Mthandizi* at length in their works titled *Competition for the Labour Supply in Mzimba District: The Case of Wenela and Mthandizi, 1906-1956*, and *The Competition for Malawian Labour, Wenela and Mthandizi in Ntcheu District, 1935-1956*, respectively.

It is worth noting that one of the advantages of emigrating through official channels was the fact that the recruiting agency took care of all the migrants' needs both *en route* and upon arrival in South Africa. Such needs not only included transport, food and accommodation, but also their health needs. It is imperative, however, that all those potential migrants who failed to emigrate through official channels resorted to the only available option: *selufu*. It is noteworthy that *selufu* involved going to South Africa largely on foot. Literature shows that *selufu* migrants could at times catch lorries between Malawi and Zimbabwe. Since under *selufu* migrants were walking for a large part of their journey, the basic question is 'what happened when one fell sick along the way?' "When one fell sick, it was a very difficult and worrying situation. Why? Because we were right in the forests" (Interview Sakala 2010).

In such circumstances, *mankhwala gha chifipa* (local medicine) became handy, as Dickson Sakala explains:

> We could try to give the patient (our friend) some local medicine which we were carrying. However, this depended on the nature and type of sickness. At times, it is sad to note, the medicine could not work and the condition deteriorated. In such a case we could temporarily stop at a place to adequately look after the patient. However, this option in itself had another complication: terrible food shortages. In this case, we relied on food handouts from nearby villages (Interview Sakala 2010).

The migrants had to brave wild animals and (incurable) diseases along the way. In case *makhwala gha chifipa* failed to cure such diseases, they resorted to medical attention, but from hospitals upon reaching South Africa. Those migrating through *selufu* could hardly use roads (hence could not access medication from hospitals) for fear of being caught by the police. That is why they preferred to go through forests. However, the unfortunate part with this option is that they could hardly get assistance along the way from well-wishers in these deserted places. It is, therefore, not surprising to note that some migrants were dying along the way from some of the sicknesses. When such a sad thing happened, migrants were quick to point out that they abandoned such a dead body as there was no time to accord one another a dignified burial in such circumstances: their lives were at great risk from captors and wild animals.

In the contemporary period, migrants also face a lot of difficulties in case of sickness *en route* to and from South Africa. The same applies to those who are deported by the South African authorities. A good case in point is John Jere (real name), who has been deported three times. During one of the trips he fell sick and sought medical attention from the hospital: "I fell sick while in jail in South Africa. I caught a bad cough and I was purging. I was taken to a hospital. Later on I was deported. I arrived home very weak. I spent a night (here) at home. The following day, I was taken to the hospital (Mzimba *boma*), where I got better after taking medication" (Interview Jere 2005).

4. Labour Migration, Diseases and Local Medicine

Tuberculosis (hereafter TB) is an infectious disease that is contracted mainly through inhalation of airborne droplets containing *tubercle bacilli* that are emitted by persons with active TB (Packard 1989: xviii). Packard argues that although TB ranks low among the communicable diseases in infectiousness per unit of time exposure, long or frequent exposure, often associated with overcrowding, may lead to a thirty percent risk of becoming infected (among case contacts). In the same vein, he further argues that "the association of TB transmission with overcrowding and of TB mobility and mortality with malnutrition, immunosuppressant infections, and physical stresses, all often associated with poverty, has made TB a classic social disease, and its incidence is thus linked to changing social and economic conditions within society" (Packard 1989: xviii).

Packard in his book *White Plague, Black Labour* has demonstrated how the migrant labour system in South Africa played a role in the transmission of urban-based TB to the rural households. The movement of migrant workers back and forth between the mines and their rural homes was actually responsible for the transmission in question. No wonder there were, reportedly, very high TB infection rates by 1920s.

In a related development, it has been indicated that, within the rural areas themselves, the risk of a TB worker infecting his family and neighbours was determined by the extent to which housing and sanitation conditions either facilitated or prevented the transmission. In this respect, Packard states that there is ample evidence that overcrowded housing was a problem in parts of the Ciskei and Transkei in South Africa during the early part of the 20th century. This is supported by cases of overcrowding among the families of returned mine workers in Pondoland, as reported by Millar:

> The overcrowding is probably worse than anything that can be found in an East End slum of a great city at home. One may see twenty people crowded into a small hut, the

door of which is carefully blocked up and which contains no other opening or ventilation of any kind. The overcrowding is very much the rule, it being the exception to find a hut not overcrowded. Now imagine the phthisical patient one of this crowd, constantly spitting on the floor and on the walls of the hut, and can it be wondered that the disease spreads? (Packard 1989: 102)

It is surprising that the disease keeps on claiming the lives of many people despite the fact that it has a cure. This is exactly the question that was posed by Doctors P. Fourie, G. Townshend and H. Kleeberg in 1985: "since TB is totally curable and available control measures are sufficient to combat the disease effectively, the natural course of the epidemic can be altered to a rapid decline. Why then does the problem remain a serious one?" (Packard 1989: xv). Among the reasons given, much of the increase in TB cases is attributed to the concurrent epidemic of HIV/AIDS that disrupts the tenuous balance between TB infection and resistance which keeps most people from ever getting TB. This is because HIV/AIDS undermines the immune systems of many women and men.

Oral evidence from Mzimba District shows that labour migrants suffered from various diseases during the migration process. Most of these were closely associated with migrants' mobility between Malawi and South Africa. Informants in the study area indicated (in unison) that Malawian healers' *mankhwala* (medicines) for treating STDs and sexually transmitted infections (STIs) have been the most popular since the 1930s and 1940s. It seems that local treatments for both STDs and STIs became highly sought after in northern Malawi as rates of infection increased following the increase in labour migration. The latter increased in the early 1940s following the resumption of official recruitment at the end of the 1930s. Oral testimony shows that STDs frequently treated by healers included *mabomu* (gonorrhea) and *chindoko* or *chizonono* (syphilis). Most informants indicated that hospitals were generally ineffective in treating these STDs, hence the popularity of *mankhwala gha chifipa*. The latter for STDs and STIs, together with *mankhwala gha mwabi* (luck medicines), were the most popular medicines administered by a healer-migrant named Dickson Sakala in the mine compounds during his migration hey-days in the 1950s (Interview Sakala 2010).

Like STDs, the condition known as *phungo* was also strongly associated with migrancy. It was believed to be a result of changes of weather or location, for instance moving to *malo ghakuzizima* (a colder environment). This is why *phungo* is, arguably, closely associated with malaria since one of the symptoms is fever. *Phungo* could affect migrants just after arrival in South Africa and upon return (back home). It is maintained that *phungo* was one of the treatable diseases and responded to both Western and African medicine. According to Landwell Jere, another healer-migrant in Zubayumo Makamo area, *phungo* is a very old disease and most healers in the area (including himself) have so far planted medicinal trees in their compounds to treat *phungo* and other ailments (Interview Jere 2009).[5]

In addition, healers in the study area indicated that they cure a whole list of migrants' illnesses: *chilaso* (pneumonia); *vilonda vya munthumbo* (stomach sores); *chikhoso* (cough); and *'mutu'* (headache). Rita Kachali, a female traditional healer in Zubayumo Makamo, sheds light on medication she prescribes for some of these diseases:

> For medicine to treat *chilaso* (pneumonia), you take a piece of maize cob together with a broom for sweeping the surroundings; there is need to burn and grind these and you apply the resultant soot on the *simbo* (cuts made on the skin). For *chikhoso*, you take roots of an okra tree (*derere*) locally

known as *nyoronyoro*; add with water and administer in liquid form; you may also, alternatively, use soya leaves or dig its roots. *Muzgakaka* (a very bitter local tree) is used to treat *'mutu'* (headache). It is prepared (ground) and administered through *simbo* (Interview Kachali 2010).[6]

However, it is worth noting that although the above prescriptions seem to be straight-forward, the reality on the ground is actually more complicated. For a lay person, you can hardly treat a particular disease despite following the above instructions in preparing medication. Surely there are other additives or processes that the healer himself or herself follows.

Furthermore, it is important to note that although most of the diseases discussed in this section such as *vilaso* (plural for *chilaso*), *phungo*, *'mutu'* and various STDs are strongly associated with labour migration, they are not considered essentially 'foreign' diseases such as TB and influenza had been in the 1920s. In general terms, diseases contracted in South Africa were seen in the same light as those contracted in Malawi. Consequently, they were in principle regarded as treatable by local healers.

5. Luck Medicines, Protection Medicines and Migrants' Stay in South Africa

Literature shows that the majority of cross-border migrants in southern Africa remain circular migrants. Put differently, although many migrants stay longer than initially intended, their visits are generally seen as temporary. This view is echoed, among others, by D. Posel, who succinctly argues that many migrants who enter South Africa continue to see themselves as circular migrants. They come to South Africa for employment or income-generating opportunities for a definite period and "have very little interest in staying in the country permanently" (Posel 2004: 6). This brings in the concept of recurrent migration where migrants purposefully emigrate to South Africa more than once. Hence circular migrants are in this case recurrent migrants. By going to and working in South Africa more than once, migrants intend to maximise proceeds from migration, yet at the same time remaining in constant touch with their households. Mr. Anthony Lupafya had this to say on the matter:

When I was going to South Africa, I did not want to stay there for a long time (i.e. overstaying). I had a clear-cut motive: to accumulate a lot within the shortest time possible and during this period maintain stable relations with my family. Whatever proceeds I was realising from my 'piece jobs' I was investing here at home, for example, buying iron sheets, fertilizer, cattle, etc. After working for a few years, I ventured into transport business and right now I am one of the reputable transporters, transporting migrants and their property between Mzimba District and South Africa (Interview Lupafya 2005).

Similarly, Dickson Sakala could not agree more with Anthony:

In our case, we used to go to South Africa in those old days under *Wenela*, *Mthandizi* or *selufu*. These days we advise our children not to overstay in South Africa. In my case, I have four sons who are currently working in South Africa. And they are doing fine - investing the proceeds from their work here at home. Consequently, they have built nice iron-roofed houses, have cars and are doing well in agriculture. Its either they come home after a brief stay or it's their wives who follow them, for instance, once a year (Interview Sakala 2005).

However, there is another dimension of recurrent migration: this is where *madipotii* are compelled to go back to South Africa at whatever cost after having been deported. Due to such deportations, migrants' stay in South Africa and their work or "piece jobs" (*maganyu*), to use their preferred term, are curtailed. The implication is that their clear-cut goals cannot be fulfilled. Consequently, filled with the burning desire and determination to accomplish their mission, *madipotii* are ready to re-emigrate using any available means. In short, their deportation is quickly followed by re-emigration which is, inadvertently, followed by yet another deportation and this becomes a cycle, hence recurrent migration.

Oral evidence shows that there is consensus among migrants in general and among *madipotii*, specifically, that deportations have a deleterious effect on the accumulation of proceeds and, consequently, on their careers. This is mainly because these deportations always come without notice and migrants have no time to put their houses in order, for example, leaving their property, including money, in the custody of their colleagues and friends. To make matters worse, they have no time to give notice of leave to their bosses, hence job losses.

Once home, in Malawi, they are actually ridiculed as "failed migrants" and that is why they quickly reprocess their trip back to South Africa. Benjamin Jere has this to say on this:

> Right now I want to embark on a project of moulding bricks for sale. I have teamed up with my friends, who also want to go to South Africa. In fact, we were just waiting for the rains to come to an end. Since I was deported, I have always been trying to find means of securing enough money to cater for my expenses on my way back to South Africa, but money is hard to come by here at home. I don't want to

stay too long, nonetheless, otherwise it's embarrassing in the eyes of the public. You need to go back as quickly as possible to continue with your mission (Interview Jere 2005).

The question which troubles the *dipotii* (deportee) is: "why is he or she susceptible to deportations unlike others?" Or put differently and generally, why are some migrants never deported while working in South Africa? This is where traditional medicinal beliefs come in. For instance, oral evidence from Zubayumo Makamo area shows that some migrants believe in use of particular *mankhwala* which effectively protects them from meeting the South Africa police in the streets. Hence the concept *kunogza ulendo* (literary, preparing the trip). This actually requires the potential migrant to adequately prepare for the intended trip, including how he or she is going to ensure a stay without deportations in South Africa. This involves consulting traditional healers or herbalists for *mankhwala gha mwabi* (luck medicine). There are notable healers in the area who are specialized in such medicine. Good examples are Linesi Mhone, a female traditional healer, and Dickson Sakala. It is not a surprise, therefore, that Dickson has four sons working in South Africa and all of them 'are doing very fine'. A visit to Dickson's home would attest to this as there are iron-roofed, 'big' houses built by his sons using proceeds from working in South Africa. In addition to *mankhwala gha mwabi*, Dickson also assists migrants with protective medicine: with the latter, migrants cannot be fired anyhow at their workplace.

One of the ex-migrants who benefited from the use of *mankhwala gha mwabi* (luck medicines) is Kingston Lupafya. His wife, Rita Kachali, is one of the renowned traditional healers in Zubayumo Makamo area. It is interesting to note that he used to get the luck medicine in question from his wife. He confessed during interviews that luck medicine really works as he kept on being highly regarded by his bosses throughout his stay in South Africa. He indicated that he stayed with one boss for a period of twenty-six years. During all this time he was a supervisor and a paymaster to his fellow employees, some of whom were whites (Interview Lupafya 2010). He further indicated that he had never been deported during the entire period he was working in South Africa. He attributes all this to the effectiveness of *mankhwala gha mwabi*.

Another interesting case is that of Trywell Mtchona Chisi, an ex-migrant who had worked in South Africa largely under *selufu* arrangement close to thirty years. Mtchona is actually his migration knick-name, which literally means 'the over-stayer'. Just like Kingston, Mtchona never got deported from South Africa:

> We would be walking in the streets with my migrant friends. Upon meeting the police, it is my friends who ended up being arrested (and eventually deported). As for me, the police could not even see me physically: I could pass by unnoticed. Do you know why this was the case? I had very effective protective medicine. I could come home for a holiday and not because of deportation. In addition, I usually got very good, well-paying jobs, for instance, as a welder, something very rare in those old days. As you are aware, most *selufu* migrants were employed in people's homes and the wages were relatively low (Interview Chisi 2005).

As a result of this, he came home a rich man by village standards. He used proceeds from working in South Africa to establish viable businesses in Zubayumo Makamo area, for instance, he owned three maize mills. He was also a very successful commercial farmer in the area.

There are some people who specialize in particular types of medicine, for instance, luck medicine and not protective

125

medicine. This means that labour migrants who get medicine from them are 'partially prepared' for work and stay in South Africa. A case in point here is Bright Jere. He is very good at *mnkhwala wakupenjera ntchito* (medicine for finding jobs), but does not deal in protective medicine. Consequently, once his son, John Jere, goes to South Africa, he easily finds employment to the extent of employers scrambling for him. This is a result of the effectiveness of the medicine he gets from his father as part of *kunozgera ulendo* (clearing the way). "When I go back to South Africa, I am sure I will not stay long before I secure another job. In fact, it may take me less than a week" (Interview Jere 2005). On this, his father, Bright, interrupts boastfully: "Finding a job in South Africa is not a problem for my son. That is not an issue. I am an expert on that (i.e. preparing luck medicine)" (Interview Jere 2005). However, while in South Africa he is prone to arrests and deportations since he lacks protective medicine. In fact, he had been deported for a total three times.

6. *Kuthwasa* (Becoming a Healer) and Labour Migration

Much of the literature has examined the relationship between traditional healing practices and medicinal beliefs, on one hand, and the church and western medicine, on the other hand. On the linkage between migration and traditional practices, the focus has been on witchcraft (Soko and Kubik 2008; Englund 2002: 137-154; Wilson 2012: 149-173). This section, however, examines *kuthwasa* as a process through which, once successful, people become healers.

Oral evidence shows that there are different types or categories of healers, for instance, the spirit- possessed (those who become healers through a process known as *kuthwasa*: falling sick and in the process being possessed by spirits and eventually leading to *vimbuza*) and the trained healers, who were trained by either their parents, other relations or by established healers. And there are some who go through the process of *kuthwasa*, but at the end fail to know the medicines for diseases despite being possessed by spirits. According to most informants, the trained healers are believed to have limited knowledge of local medicine.

In the 1940s there were renowned healers in the study area, for example, Morton Moyo, Gray Sakala and Gaga Makamo. These were healers who relied on dancing (*vimbuza*) for them to get charged before administering local medicine (Soko and Kubik 2008; Hokkanen 2007: 733-750). It is worth noting that there are other spirit-possessed healers who practice their trade without dancing, whereas the third category combines both aspects: dancing and not-dancing. During the old migration days, there were some Malawian healers who were practicing in South Africa. These healers had Malawi Government certificates which were recognized in South Africa because they bore official (government) stamps. They used to carry prepared (ground) medicine (in powder form) which they administered to patients in South Africa. Whenever they ran out of stocks, they used to come home for replenishment. It is worth noting that there were equally indigenous healers in South Africa. However, whenever they failed to cure diseases, most people (including South African nationals) turned to healers from Malawi for assistance. This was mainly because of the trust they had in *mankhwala* from Malawi.[7]

One of the healers who underwent *kuthwasa* (*uthwasi*) is Linesi Mhone and she narrates her experience:

> I was born in 1963 and after I got married (1979), I fell sick. They took me to several hospitals, but to no avail. Later on they took me to a traditional healer where it was discovered that I had *vinthenda/ vimbuza* (spirits). Thereafter I

discovered that I started to know, through spirits, *mankhwala* for various diseases. That is how I started attending to people (the sick) until later on I started to have in-patients at my place. If a patient is sick because he or she was bewitched *'nkhununa'* (I do screen the patient through my spirits until I identify the problem) (Interview Mhone 2010).

Linesi argues that there are good working relations between healers and medical doctors in the hospitals. Whenever healers come across conditions requiring the attention of medical doctors, they do not hesitate to refer such cases to hospitals. The opposite is also true. As healers, they get referral cases from hospitals on a regular basis. Most of such cases involve witchcraft.

A more extreme case of *kuthwasa* is that of Dickson Sakala who became a full-fledged healer after years of working in South Africa:

> In 1984 I was filled with *vinthenda* (spirits) and through them I stayed six months without eating *sima* (Malawi's staple dish). During this period I was eating *nkhazi, nthuma, chinthembwe,* and *mwazaghamba* (very bitter, wild herbs). These spirits showed me 397 local trees (traditional medicine) which I use to heal the sick. This is how I became a healer (Interview Mhango 2009).

Dickson, whose practice name is Viyezgo (temptations), narrated that he uses a fly whisk, a baton stick and a piece of cloth inscribed 'Viyezgo' when administering medicine to clients. Although he is a *vimbuza*-type healer, at times he does his job without drum beating in the background.[8]

Although Dickson had *kuthwasa* experience in the 1980s, he had been practicing as a healer way before this experience. He used to go to South Africa to work in the mines. There he was staying in mine compounds. He used

128

to carry along *mankhwala gha chifipa* and used to assist or heal other migrants whenever they fell sick. However, he was quick to point out that *mankhwala ghakagwirisikanga ntchito mchibisibisi* (local medicine was administered secretly).

When migrants fell sick while working in South Africa, they used to be treated using both Western medicine and *mankhwala gha chifipa* (local medicine). Most migrants used to carry local medicine with them in powdered form. However, there were certain conditions which could not be treated in South Africa, for example, *kuthwasa*. With this condition, a sick migrant had to be repatriated home in order to get adequate medical attention from the *sing'anga*. The sick person could be given different types of medication until the process of kuthwasa was complete. The end result would be *vimbuza* (spirit possession) in which the person would end up knowing *mankhwala* for various diseases, hence becoming a *sing'anga*. This person would either stay at home and start practicing or go to South Africa to work and to practice, hence healer-migrant. If, on the other hand, the person is only healed from the sickness, i.e. did not have *vimbuza*, then he or she could not become a *sing'anga*.

7. Conclusion

The chapter has established the close relationship between local medicine and labour migration both during the old and contemporary migration periods. For instance, it has shown that because of the strict recruitment process by *Wenela*, some migrants resorted to using *mankhwala gha chifipa* in order to ensure that they got engaged. It has also shown that most *selufu* migrants relied on *mankhwala gha chifipa* on their way to and from South Africa as they could not visit hospitals for fear of being apprehended by the police.

The chapter has shown that there were a number of diseases which were associated with the mobility of labour migrants. In this connection, the chapter argues that there were diseases that could be treated by both Western medicine and local medicine. Examples here are various STDs and STIs, excluding HIV/AIDS which still does not have a cure. However, in addition to these, it has been indicated, there were particular local diseases like *kuthwasa* which could effectively be treated by local medicine only.

Using human agency school, the chapter argues that labour migrants and healer-migrants are rational and purposive individuals. They are determined to achieve their set goals by 'surmounting obstacles' through the use of *mankhwala gha chifipa*. The chapter concludes that particular types of local medicines, for example, *mankhwala gha mwabi* and protective medicines are important not only in securing jobs, but also for the migrants' continued stay at their destination (South Africa) in the face of arrests and deportations by the South African police. Lastly, the chapter has examined the complex process of *kuthwasa* and the pivotal roles played by the healers in the entire labour migration process.

References

Banda, H.C.C. (2000) 'Competition for the Labour Supply in Mzimba District: The Case of *Wenela* and *Mthandizi*, 1906-1956', History Department, Zomba, Chancellor College, University of Malawi.

Banda, H.C.C. 2008 'Gendered Patterns of Malawian Contemporary Migrancy: The Case of Zubayumo Makamo Area in Mzimba District, 1970s-2005' (Unpublished MA Thesis), History Department, Chancellor College, Zomba.

Banda, H.C.C. 2011 '*Madipotii*: International Recurrent Migrants from Zubayumo Makamo area during the Contemporary Migration Period' (Unpublished Paper), Mzuzu University, Mzuzu.

Boeder, R.B. (1973) 'The Effects of Labour Emigration on Rural Life in Malawi', *Rural Africana*, Michigan State University.

Bozzoli, B. (1983) 'Marxism, Feminism and South African Studies', *Journal of South African Studies*, 9, 2, 139-171.

Chirwa, W.C. (1992) "TEBA is Power': Rural Labour, Migrancy and Fishing in Malawi, 1890s-1985', PhD Thesis, Queens University, Kingston, Ontario.

Englund, Harri (2002) 'The Village in the City, the City in the Village: Migrants in Lilongwe', *Journal of Southern African Studies*, 28, 1, 137-154.

Groves, Zoe (2011) 'Malawians in Colonial Salisbury: A Social History of Migration in Central Africa, c. 1920s-1960s' (PhD Thesis), Keele University.

Hokkanen, M. and Banda, H.C.C. (2013) 'Migrant Workers, Mobile Medicines: Mobility, Labour and Medical Culture in Northern Malawi' (Unpublished Research Paper), Mzuzu University, Mzuzu.

Hokkanen, Markku (2007) 'Quests for Health and Contests for Meaning: African Church Leaders and Scottish Missionaries in the Early Twentieth Century Presbyterian Church in Northern Malawi', *Journal of Southern African Studies*, 33, 4, 733-750.

Hokkanen, Markku (2004) 'Scottish Missionaries and African Healers: Perceptions and Relations in the Livingstonia Mission, 1875-1930', *Journal of Religion in Africa*, 34 (3), 1-28.

Nkhoma, B. G. (1995) 'The Competition for Malawian Labour: *Wenela* and *Mthandizi* in Ntcheu, 1935-1956', History Department, Zomba, Chancellor College.

Pachai, B. (1973) *Malawi: The History of the Nation*, London: Longman.

Packard, R. (1989) *White Plague, Black Labour: Tuberculosis and the Political Economy of Health Disease in Africa*, Berkeley: University of California Press.

Posel, D. (2001) 'Have Migration Patterns in Post-Apartheid South Africa Changed?' Unpublished paper, 6.

Sanderson, F.E. (1961) 'The Development of Labour Migration from Nyasaland, 1891-1914', *Journal of African History*, 14, 2, 1961, 259-271.

Soko, Boston and Kubik, Gerhard (2008) *Nchimi Chikanga: The Battle against Witchcraft in Malawi*, Zomba: Kachere Series.

Wendroff, A.P. 'Care and Social Change: The Case of Northern Malawi', in J.H. Morgan, J.H. (ed.) *Third World Medicine and Social Change: A Reader in Social Science and Medicine*, New York: University Press of America.

Wilson, Anita (2012) 'Of Love Potions and Witch Baskets: Domesticity, Mobility and Occult Rumours in Malawi', *Western Folklore*, 71, 2, 149-173.

Primary Sources
Archival Sources
MNA S 36/1/2/6: Female immigration into South Africa.

Oral Interviews
Anthony Lupafya, Zubayumo Makamo Village, Mzimba, 18/04/2005.

Benjamin Jere, Kazezani Makamo Village, Mzimba, 27/04/2005.

Bright Jere, Kazezani Makamo Village, Mzimba, 29/04/2005.

Dickson Sakala, Zubayumo Makamo Village, Mzimba, 20/06/2010.

John Jere, Kazezani Makamo Village, Mzimba, 29/04/2005.

Kigston Lupafya, Zubayumo Makamo Village, Mzimba, 19/06/2010.

Landwell Jere, Kazezani Makamo Village, Mzimba, 16/07/2009.

Linesi Mhone, Zebediya Makamo, Mzimba, 20/06/2010.

Rita Kachali, Zubayumo Makamo Village, Mzimba, 19/06/2010.

Trywell Chisi, Zebediya Makamo Village, Mzimba, 27/04/2005

Winstead Lupafya, Zubayumo Makamo Village, Mzimba, 17/04/2005.

Notes

[1] The first version of this paper was presented during the "Moving Bodies" Workshop at the African Centre for Migration and Society (ACMS) at the University of the Witwatersrand, 16th-19th September 2014.

[2] These areas have not been listed in order of importance of labour emigration. It is worth noting that these areas are very popular in the district. If one went to Mzimba *boma* and tried to find out about the migration areas in the district, he or she is bound to come across such areas. However, it should not be a surprise to learn that some migrants come from other areas since Mzimba District is generally a labour migration area.

[3] Most writers have written on the failure by the Nyasaland (later Malawi) Government to control *selufu*.

[4] The frequent deportations of migrants are another interesting aspect of contemporary migration. Evidence from Zubayumo Makamo area shows that some migrants have prospered after being deported for, say, three times. For details on *madipotii*, see chapter four.

[5] When I visited Landwell, he showed me some of the medicinal trees which he planted as a solution to the scarcity of local medicinal trees, not only in the study area, but in Malawi generally. This scarcity is a result of deforestation and environmental desiccation.

[6] Rita Kachali's husband, Kingston Lupafya, greatly relied on use of medicines during his labour migration days.

[7] In January 2015 while in Johannesburg I was approached by a South African lady, who had learnt I was from Malawi: "I hear you are

from Malawi; may you give me some contacts of Malawian healers based here in Johannesburg. Malawian healers are renowned for effective local medicine", she insisted.

[8] Most healers indicated that they usually have a day in a week when they conduct full-fledged *vimbuza* with drum beating.

Chapter 7

Conclusion

This book is a collection of the different perspectives on the nature of labour migration from Mzimba, one of the major labour migration districts in Malawi. Mzimba District is unique in many respects. The people in the district, the Ngoni, originated and emigrated from *Zululand* and fled from the troubled spot during the *Mfecane*. Between the 1820s and 1850s they moved northwards through present-day Mozambique, Zambia and Malawi till they reached Tanzania. Here they experienced a second, but small-scale dispersal which saw the Ngoni drifting back, southwards, to parts of northern Malawi (Mzimba District) and central Malawi (Dedza and Ntcheu districts). It is not surprising, therefore, that the Ngoni of Malawi took advantage of the labour migration process to go to South Africa since to them this meant 'going back to our roots'.

The substantive chapters in the book examine different themes under both old and new labour migration periods. These themes include competition for the labour supply, gendered nature of labour migration, xenophobia; recurrent migration, and the role of medicine behind migration. The book fervently shows that the Ngoni of Mzimba have been ardent participants in the labour migration history since the beginning of the 20th century. Since *Wenela* established its recruitment station in Mzimba District, the Ngoni were compelled to emigrate formally under it. Following the introduction of *Mthandizi* recruitment operations for the Zimbabwean farms, the Ngoni later started exercising a choice either to emigrate under *Wenela* or *Mthandizi*. This development, as chapter two shows, brought about fierce competition for labour between these two recruiting bodies.

It would, therefore, be proper to conclude that, based on evidence presented in the book, the Ngoni largely emigrated under formal migration (unlike under *selufu*) during the old labour migration period.

Following the curtailment of labour recruitment operations in Malawi first by *Mthandizi* (for the Zimbabwean farms) and then by *Wenela* and lastly by *Theba* (for the South African mines), one would have expected labour migration to come to a grinding halt. However, the continuation of this migration under *selufu*, albeit on a grander scale, into the 1990s and beyond shows that labour migration is 'a lifeblood' for a cross-section of Malawians, especially the Ngoni from Mzimba District. Unlike other ethnic groups in Malawi, for instance, the Tumbuka from Rumphi district, the Ngonde from Karonga district, the Chewa from central Malawi, and the Yao and the Lhomwe from southern Malawi, who are able to look for other income-generating avenues within the country, for the Ngoni of Mzimba, and especially those in the core migration areas, emigrating to South Africa is but 'a way of life'. That is why, as chapter three shows, even women joined the labour migration process following the collapse of apartheid and the introduction of democratic governance both in South Africa and Malawi in 1994.

Chapters four and five have, collectively, unveiled the difficult circumstances under which Malawian labour migrants operate while in South Africa. It is worth noting that these challenges are faced by immigrants from various countries, for example, Mozambique and Zimbabwe, the other two traditional labour suppliers to South Africa. By focusing on the 2008 xenophobic attacks, the book shows that working informally in South Africa is not rosy at all: the migrants' stay is a matter of life and death. Chapter five focuses on the frequent arrests and deportations of illegal Malawian migrants in South Africa. However, due to the determination of *madipotii* (i.e. deportees), these deportations

136

are followed by *madipotii* quickly reprocessing their journeys back to South Africa, in the process ushering in recurrent migration. Chapter six is related to chapters four and five in that it examines the migrants' ways of dealing with challenges in South Africa. After being pushed to the extremes by such challenges, some labour migrants have no option but to resort to the use of *mankhwala gha chifipa*. The chapter highlights the role of luck medicine and protective medicine in this ordeal.

Appendix

"Chiuta ngwa Lusungu" (God is Merciful): Most of the names of the shops and booking offices at *Mzimba boma* (such as this one) show clearly that the owners (in this case transporters) are filled with hope – that their businesses will succeed. As can be seen from the picture, this serves not only as a booking office to South Africa, but also as an outlet (shop) for various South African quality products (e.g. chair and floor mats).

Most booking offices at *Mzimba boma* have both Malawian and South African cell phone numbers as one way of instilling trust in potential migrants. The latter can either talk directly to transporters (using South African numbers) or their shrewd agents based permanently in Malawi.

Most young men in Mzimba District will embark on anything that guarantees them monetary rewards with which they would prepare their journeys down to "*Jobeki*" (Joburg for Johannesburg). A good example of such initiatives (embarkations) is land clearing and tilling (locally known as *magadi*), as shown in this picture, in readiness of the ensuing crop growing season.

In the olden days the 'road to South Africa' was rough (as illustrated by this road here) and the migrants actually had to travel on foot due to lack of means of transport. Consequently, they were embarking on what would be termed as step migration, that is, migrating in phases, stopping over in Zambia and Zimbabwe *en route* to their final destination, South Africa.

Nowadays the journey to South Africa is made simple by a network of good tar marc roads right from the migrants' origin, Mzimba *boma*, to their destination, Johannesburg. In addition to the good road network, there is a variety of means of transport e.g. pick-up lorries and coaches plying transport business between the two migration areas. In Zubayumo Makamo area a number of migrants who 'graduated' from working in people's homes in South Africa are now into this transport business.

Although Mzimba District is renowned for precious stones, gemstones, in northern Malawi, as depicted in this picture, not many people are into mining. One obvious reason is lack of capital outlay required for such an undertaking. As a result the majority join the popular migration process. In fact, for a cross-section of these migrants, migrating to South Africa is 'a way of earning a better living!'

Chibaya cha mbuzi (a traditional goat kraal): A visit to a number of households in Mzimba District reveals that most households nowadays do not own livestock like cattle, goats and pigs. This is a sign of impoverishment at household and societal level. This was not the case in the past. This is partly the reason why it is rather difficult for would-be migrants to process their way to South Africa. However, the migration areas boast of embarking on rearing of such livestock using part of the proceeds from working in South Africa, hence an indication of economic transformation. In addition, during the multi-party era there are a number of NGOs distributing goats in various districts including Mzimba as part of the process of gradually empowering the rural communities.

Printed in the United States
By Bookmasters